W0115411
9780874621020

ST. THOMAS
AND THE GENTILES

PRINTED AT THE MARQUETTE UNIVERSITY PRESS
MILWAUKEE, WISCONSIN

MORTIMER J. ADLER

Portrait in Profile by Maude Phelps Hutchins

The Aquinas Lecture 1938

SAINT THOMAS AND THE GENTILES

Under the Auspices of the Aristotelian Society of Marquette University

BY

MORTIMER J. ADLER
Associate Professor of the Philosophy of Law, University of Chicago

MILWAUKEE
MARQUETTE UNIVERSITY PRESS
1938

MILWAUKEE
MARQUETTE UNIVERSITY PRESS

PERMISSU SUPERIORUM

THE AQUINAS LECTURES

The Aristotelian Society of Marquette University each year invites a scholar to speak on the philosophy of St. Thomas Aquinas. These lectures have come to be called the Aquinas Lectures and are customarily delivered on the Sunday nearest March seven, the feast day of the Society's patron saint.

This year the Aristotelian Society has the pleasure of recording the lecture of Dr. Mortimer J. Adler, associate professor of the philosophy of law in the University of Chicago since 1930. Dr. Adler was instructor in psychology in Columbia University, 1923-1929, assistant director of the People's Institute, New York City, 1928-1929, and has been visiting lecturer at St. John's College, Annapolis, Maryland since 1937. As a member of the Thomistic Institute of America and of many other learned societies he has forcefully defended the cause of Thomistic philosophy. Among his publications are *Dialectic* (New York, 1927), *Crime, Law and Social Science,* in collaboration with Prof. Jerome Michael (New York, 1933), *Art and Prudence* (New York, 1937), and *What Man Has Made of Man* (New York, 1937). To this list the Aristotelian Society has the honor of adding *St. Thomas and the Gentiles.*

St. Thomas and the Gentiles

I.

In the sixty years which have elapsed since the encyclical *Aeterni Patris,* the study and teaching of the philosophy of St. Thomas Aquinas have been pursued with increasing vigor. In works of exposition and commentary, in polemical tracts against adversaries, in countless panegyrics which have rivalled each other to reach the summit of praise, and even in attempts, necessarily fewer in number, to supplement or extend the doctrine itself, ample evidence has been given of the vitality of a philosophy which dared to be called perennial. It would be pleasant for us to celebrate the name and work of St. Thomas by rejoicing in these manifestations. We could do no more than repeat, of course, what has already been often repeated by voices more eloquent than ours and speaking from a fuller vision than we have attained. If I depart from this procedure, it is not from a wish to avoid reiteration, for that necessarily occurs when the members of a community express to each other their common sentiments and devotions. It is rather because I cannot help thinking of the larger company of men who have heard the clearest voices, but have not heeded. If they have read St. Thomas or what has been written in his tradition, they have not discovered why it is that we rejoice. On the contrary, the praises which might arise here would not re-echo in other corridors of learning. We would be deaf if we did not hear a reverberation of a different sort, an answering cry of dissidence, almost vituperation. Let us forego, then, the pleasure of congratulating ourselves on this anniversary of the teacher to whom we hold all men should be disciples, to ask the unpleasant question whether our discipleship has been at fault.

I would first be sure that you are acquainted with the facts which cause me to invite you to join in this course of self-examination. Otherwise, failing to see the ground for it, you might dismiss my concern as unduly morose. I am, perhaps, more conversant with such facts than others, because I come from a university where the feeling against St. Thomas is out of all proportion to the effort which has been made in his behalf. This is not an isolated phenomenon. Wherever in the secular universities there has been a revival of interest in mediaeval philosophy, leading inevitably to an enthusiasm for St. Thomas, it was not long before another renaissance occurred, a revival of the cries against scholasticism, authoritarian dogmatism, the anti-scientific spirit, metaphysical verbalism, an out-moded formal logic, and a puerile subservience to antiquity, especially the scheme of Aristotelian categories. We must not be allowed to forget that all the values most prized by modern men were won by a struggle against the decadent scholasticism of the 15th and 16th centuries. The sudden threat of Thomism quite naturally awakens the passions which preceded the birth of modern times. If we are surprised at the vehemence with which the spirit of the Renaissance reasserts itself to prevent any backsliding, it can only be because we had not understood our allegiance to St. Thomas as a signal for backsliding. In the name of St. Thomas we should be even more opposed than Francis Bacon, David Hume and the rest to the corrupt scholastics of the Renaissance, with their logic-chopping and their senseless opposition to the findings of scientific research. It is we, not St. Thomas, who have been misunderstood, and the fault is ours. We must not permit ourselves to suppose that the contemporary reaction has been occasioned by a fresh reading of the Thomistic texts. They along with other great works of ancient and mediaeval philosophy are read less, and less carefully, by our contemporaries than they were by the founders of modern thought. No, the reaction has been caused by queer persons, like myself, who have become acquainted with the wisdom of St. Thomas and, with almost romantic excitement, have been unguarded in their declarations. We have seen with a lover's eye and spoken with his unreserve. We have appeared as so many Don Quixotes proclaiming the beauty of Dulcinea del Toboso to a world that could see only an ugly hag being snatched from the grave.

The essential paradox of this situation can be expressed in many contrasts, confronting us on all sides. We who have thought that we were bringing light from a source which the modern world had needlessly neglected are charged with obscurantism. Is it possible that we defeated our purpose by speaking the words of ages still generally regarded as dark? We who learned from St. Thomas that man knows reality by means of many operations [1], of which philosophy is only one, certainly must have realized the limitations of philosophy, bounded, on the one hand, by the autonomous sphere of faith and, on the other, by the apparently autonomous province of empirical science. Knowing so well that the first task of the wise man is to put things in order according to their distinctions [2], we could scarcely have wished to confuse the diverse realms of knowledge, to have the philosopher answer scientific questions and be told how to answer them by religious dogma. Yet that seems to be the impression we have given in many quarters. Despite the fact that the Church, responsive to St. Thomas's ordering of faith and reason, has always refused to convert any humanly contrived doctrine into dogma,—honoring the work of St. Thomas as the best philosophy, but philosophy withal and hence forever open to argument,—despite this fact, Thomists have not succeeded in preventing their philosophy from being regarded as a religious creed [3]. We who admire St. Thomas's mastery of the art of intellectual debate,—his dialectical fecundity in posing objections to his own positions as well as in answering them, his scruple in demonstrating only what can be demonstrated, his patient skill in wrestling with errors for the sake of the truth they contain, his prudence in achieving the eminent mean which reconciles opposite extremes,—we must nevertheless be inept in the practice of his method. Had we been better imitators, should we have failed so utterly to make our dialectic felt? Could we be charged with not joining issue, with begging the question, with all sorts of arbitrariness and all manner of trickery? Finally, in calling ourselves Thomists we have thought only to declare our devotion to the cause of philosophy itself, to the truth which is above the partisan claims of divisive schools. But we find that we are regarded as belonging to a cult, to a movement dangerously subversive of the prevailing culture. Thomism is not the proper name for philosophy in its perennial vitality. It is just one ism among many, and an anachronism at that.

There is one thing in all this that tends to mitigate our fault. No matter how perfected our rhetoric, no matter how improved our dialectical skill, we could never avoid making plain what we honestly believe, namely, that St. Thomas spoke a great deal of philosophical truth, that it is still true and probably always will be. We must make this plain because this, and nothing else, is our central contention. But this, and nothing else, is also the stumbling block over which there seems to be no way of lifting the contemporary world. The notion that there is philosophical truth, the notion that such truth survives a change of culture and endures through centuries of scientific progress,—the first of these alone is a hazardous proposal; the second verges on the preposterous. And if we add, as indeed we must, that we think this enduring body of truths is not just one system of philosophy among many, but that it is philosophy itself, in which all men can share, then we ought to expect the consequence,—the charge of totalitarianism, of fascism, of seeking to impose our will upon mankind. Once this suspicion is aroused, there is little use of protesting that philosophy is the work of reason, that no doctrine can be imposed upon a mind without ceasing to be philosophy. Those on the road to dictatorship have been known to use such wiles before.

Lest you suppose that I am exaggerating, let me expand upon this point a bit further. The learned world is able to unite in praise of Shakespeare as a universal poet, but they cannot join us in praising St. Thomas as a philosopher for all men and all times. In the polite society of savants, his genius is as readily recognized as that of Shakespeare; but in the case of a philosopher, the attribution of genius is equivocal praise unless it means attainment of the truth. The equivocation takes many forms: St. Thomas created the magnificent *mediaeval* synthesis; his work was an almost perfect intellectual *system,* as intricate in design as the façade of a Gothic cathedral. Whatever propriety there is in such eulogies,—and I, for one, would challenge the use of the word "system" and the Gothic analogy,—we ought not to be deceived by even the best intentions they convey. For at their best, they do not extend to the point at which real praise begins: the achievement of an abiding truth. Thus, for example, in 1924, on the occasion of the 600th anniversary of the canonization of Thomas Aquinas, Professor A. E. Taylor, eminent both as a scholar and a philosopher, attempted to dispel misconceptions about the Angelic Doctor which he felt still persisted in the minds of cultivated Englishmen [4]. Had he talked only of St. Thomas's great learning, of his rare gifts of speculative courage and intellectual prudence; had he only removed the prevalent notion, that St. Thomas was neither original nor critical, by showing how he resisted those who spoke in the name of Aristotle when they did not speak truly, Professor Taylor might have discharged his obligation as a celebrant within the bounds of scholarship. But he went further. He dared to suggest not only that St. Thomas had accomplished a greater work of philosophical truth than Plato, Aristotle and all their other followers up to his time, but also that that truth is still alive and compares most favorably with anything done since his day [5]. Even the high scholarly reputation of Professor Taylor could not support such excessive praise, nor prevent the consequence. I make bold to suggest that from that day onward Professor Taylor was regarded by his colleagues as a trifle queer, not altogether sound in philosophical judgment, however unblemished his record as an historian.

Recently, as you know, Professor Gilson has given two brilliant series of lectures. The first of these established the thesis that the philosophical achievement of the middle ages exceeded, within the domain of reason itself, the truths attained by antiquity; and further that this achievement is rightly regarded as Christian philosophy because it occurred under the inspiration of Christian faith [6]. Outside of Catholic circles these Gifford Lectures were received with the admiration usually accorded Professor Gilson's immense scholarship, but the thesis was not seriously pondered. In fact, the thesis that mediaeval philosophy was Christian could be readily accepted, but not in the sense in which it was advanced; it merely confirmed the modern prejudice that mediaeval philosophy was all right where it belonged, namely in the middle ages. In the William James Lectures at Harvard, Professor Gilson attempted to overcome the historicism which had, in effect, vitiated the philosophical force of his earlier work. He tried to show how the history of philosophy makes philosophical sense, how, in its light, "not only philosophical truth, but even philosophical error, becomes intelligible." In reaching "those necessary connections of ideas which are philosophy itself, history automatically overcomes both itself and historicism" [7].

But, as the reviews are beginning to show, the contemporary world is still willing to applaud M. Gilson's work as an historian and a scholar, but is not so ready to follow him in penetrating through the history of philosophy to philosophy itself. It is not because these lectures contain an unanswerable indictment of the divagations of modern thought. Gilson puts salve upon that wound by an equally merciless exposé of mediaeval failures and by imputing the same round of errors to the hellenistic period of antiquity. Nor are Gilson's critics, for the most part, dismayed to discover that the history of philosophy contains so many errors, so endlessly repeated; in fact, they had always suspected as much and are glad for his confirmation and the brilliance of his wit and mockery. But, unfortunately, Gilson's intention carried him further. Against the moving background of misdirection and frustration, he hoped to show the permanence of philosophical truth, though its outlines emerge clearly for only a few moments in the course of history. More than that, he had even dared to insinuate in a few passages, and say boldly in fewer, that Plato, Aristotle, and, pre-eminently, Aquinas were the light of intelligence in the comedy of errors he had sketched. They were truly philosophers simply because they knew how to speak the philosophical truth. At this point all of M. Gilson's scholarship, brilliance, and wit availed him nothing. One reviewer of his book [8] concludes by saying: "*Despite differences which readers may feel with the author's beliefs,* they will find the book a rarely provocative and refreshing one" (italics mine). And another, a professor of philosophy at the University of Wisconsin, became more articulate than most of his colleagues would be in expressing the same point of view, namely, that what Gilson had done in dismissing other thinkers as loci of historical error applied even more drastically to Plato, Aristotle, and St. Thomas. This review was well entitled "The Error of Philosophy," because according to its writer the very idea of philosophy pretending to be knowledge of the real world, yet independent of science, is a most egregious error [9].

If these examples are not sufficient to support my point, there are many more at hand.

I shall content myself, however, with citing further only the case of Jacques Maritain. You and I who have learned so much from him,— not only about the thought of St. Thomas, but about the way in which to throw Thomistic light upon contemporary problems of nature, society, and art, — we know that M. Maritain is no copyist, faithfully transcribing the mediaeval jargon; we know that beneath the fervor of his rhetoric, his piety and zeal, there is everywhere the cold edge of analysis cutting through to the mysteries of being, so far as they are intelligible to man. But let us not, through our devotion to him, deceive ourselves about the acceptance of his work outside the narrow circle of those who share with him, initially, a common ground. He has always received less of a hearing than Gilson for the simple reason that he has been, from the beginning, more explicit in his insistence upon the point which Gilson reached in his last lecture. He is generally dismissed as an official Thomist, an apologist for a strange doctrine that he and a few others are trying to foist upon the contemporary scene. In America he is scarcely recognized in good philosophical society, except, perhaps, as the persistent representative of the other half who live across the tracks. Nor let it be thought that his high strain of impassioned oratory,—which I think he justly permits himself to enjoy,—is the sole or sufficient cause of his being frowned upon by the reigning élite whose thought runs not so deep in the roots of their being. No, the explanation is rather Maritain's unrelenting claim that philosophy is knowledge of the real, independent of and superior to empirical and mathematical science; that it is subject to an inward progress, different from the advancing movement of science by external additions; that accordingly it is perennial in conserving truth once attained, yet at the same time keeping that truth alive and ever able to grow [10]. This is Maritain's understanding of being a Thomist. This is the reason why his audience is limited.

The problem we face is clear. We have too long been proceeding as if our task were to show that the thought of St. Thomas is the best expression of what is perennially true in philosophy. That task has now been sufficiently well done. But its fruits are enjoyed only by an inner circle. We have done nothing for all those who are not really concerned with the claims of Thomism because they reject the notion that there is any abiding philosophical truth. We speak vain words when we talk of *philosophia perennis* if we are talking to those, and they are many, who relegate philosophy of any sort to the invidious status of arm-chair speculation or running commentary on the changing positive sciences. And if we cannot talk to our modern friends about philosophical knowledge, how much less intelligible we are when we mention metaphysics, the knowledge of being, and first principles [11].

I have tried to suggest that the responsibility for the reaction against Thomism is our own. I have suggested that our rhetoric may not be well-advised, that our phraseology may be obscure, even offensive, that our dialectical skill may be unequal to the task. But I wish now to place the blame in terms of our essential failure. Quite apart from the merits of Thomism as a special accomplishment, our primary obligation was to make a case for philosophy in the contemporary world. The burden of proof was upon us, and we have failed so far. Until every effort has been made, until every device has been strenuously tried and patiently exhausted, it is no defence to say that those who will not see cannot be shown. In this case I do not think we can say with Maritain, when we undertake to explain to our contemporaries "the necessity of taking St. Thomas for a teacher," that we are there "only to tell them so, not to persuade them in spite of themselves" [12]. In this case, the question is, by our own light, thoroughly arguable, and argue it we must. We are not justified in excusing ourselves by judging the others as wilfully and obstinately blind. If, as St. Augustine tells us, the highest form of charity toward men is teaching [13], can the teacher be one who is not willing to treat his disciples as men of good will, so long as human forbearance is possible? What holds for the teacher holds equally for the philosopher and his adversary. Even if he suspects that the difficulty lies in certain intractable prejudices, his withdrawal from the argument is an admission that he has not been able to give reasons in such a way that prejudice is overcome.

I am not counselling the patience of Job because, in a sense, no man deserves that much at our hands. I am not minimizing the variety of stubborn prejudices against which, it often seems to us, we have to contend [14]. I am not even above expressing the suspicion, in the light of evidences difficult to ignore, that we are not always met with good will [15]. I am only saying that there is first the mote in our own eye. We have not seen the problem clearly. Far from making every effort to join issue with those who differ from us, we have, in my judgment, not even begun to make an effort properly directed and properly proportioned to the task at hand. We have been loath to absent ourselves from the felicity of moving further into the interior of philosophical thought, when there is pressing work to be done on the border, the arduous and lowly work of the pioneer. The borderland I speak of is marked by the issue between those who hold, as we do, that philosophy is a field of knowledge in which there can be perennial truth and those who deny it.

I know of no attempt on the part of Thomists to face this issue in a way that is proportionate to the need of their adversaries for patient dialectic, the answering of all objections, the offering of all possible arguments in forms which they will not think beg the question [16]. At this point St. Thomas sets us an example we would do well to follow. I am thinking of the *Summa Contra Gentiles,* especially in contrast to the *Summa Theologica.* We have been working with the latter as our model and then wondering why the gentiles of the present day are unmoved, except in the opposite direction. We can cherish the hope of re-working the *Summa Theologica* in forms appropriate to our age, but our immediate obligation is to do the work of the *Contra Gentiles.* I like to think that it is not an historical accident that St. Thomas wrote the *Summa Contra Gentiles* first. The pioneer work should come first. If, as St. Thomas says, "it belongs to the wise man to meditate and disseminate truth" and also "to refute contrary falsehood" [17], I propose that such labors begin at the point where the need is greatest. In what follows I shall try to outline my view of the problems presented to us by the 20th-century gentiles, in the light of the analogy provided by the work of St. Thomas in behalf of the gentiles of his day.

II.

It is necessary first to measure the analogy which has suggested itself by noting the points of similarity and difference between the present situation and that of the 13th century. We can then estimate the difficulties which confront us and plan to meet them fairly.

The similitude may not be readily discerned. To one interested as St. Thomas was in expounding Christian theology, two audiences presented themselves. There were, on the one hand, those who shared with him the articles of Christian faith; and, on the other, there were the gentiles, those who were not Christians. Pre-eminently for St. Thomas the gentiles were the Moors, who partook of Christian revelation in no particular; but, by an extension of meaning, the gentiles can be thought of as including the Jews, who shared the Old Testament with Christians, and even heretics who have departed from Christianity in some dogmatic truth [18]. I shall employ this more inclusive meaning subsequently.

Here I shall consider only the case of the Moors. The project which St. Thomas undertook in the *Summa Contra Gentiles* was to argue for the truths of the Christian religion without at any point relying upon faith or appealing to the dogmas of the Church. As you know, this was accomplished by using philosophical truth as a common ground from which to proceed. The Arabs were philosophers in the same sense as the Latins, having the same tradition of philosophical learning and respecting the same techniques for arriving at the truth. This was sufficient both for intelligible communication and for profitable controversy; it was not necessary that, initially, St. Thomas and the Moors should agree on all points of doctrine.

From the point of view of Christian theology, the gentiles are essentially the same today as they were in the 13th century. They are pagans and infidels of all sorts, most of whom are not as learned of course, as the Moors St. Thomas addressed. But we are not concerned with the propagation of the faith. It is from the point of view of philosophy that we are trying to locate the gentiles of the 20th century. By analogy they must be those who share with us no part of philosophical truth. As the Moors made their position plain by denying the Christian revelation, so our gentiles separate themselves clearly from us by denying that there is any such thing as true philosophical knowledge in which they could share.

Two questions at once arise. The first question is, Were there any philosophical gentiles of this sort in the 13th century? I answer, subject to scholarly correction, that if there were, they could only have been extreme skeptics or extreme mystics, denying that there was any natural human knowledge of the general characteristics of the real world. The second question is, Are there any today? I can answer this in the affirmative, without the aid of scholarship. There are a great many and, of these, few are either skeptics or mystics in the extreme sense. It is not that they deny the possibility or existence of natural human knowledge, but rather that they combine the affirmation of science with the denial of any other kind of knowledge of the nature of things in general. By science we understand, of course, only such knowledge as is obtained by one or another sort of empirical research or investigation. If philosophy is not that, and I think we agree that it is not, then philosophy is not valid knowledge [19]. Further, now, if we include those who while they refrain from calling philosophy nonsense treat it as a field of speculation about unanswerable questions or about questions that will presently be answered by scientific method, or even as a kind of synthetic and logistic commentary on the present state of scientific knowledge, the number of the gentiles swells. Finally, if we add those who regard philosophy as a kind of knowledge which in some way depends on the contingent findings of empirical science [20], then the position of the gentiles almost becomes identical with the point of view of contemporary culture in western Europe. To make the issue clear, let me formulate the position which all gentiles, however diverse in other respects, concur in denying [21]. It is that philosophy is a body of knowledge, not obtained by any of the specialized methods of empirical research, and consisting of truths which are not dependent for their validity upon the findings of science.

It would be fitting to name the position of the contemporary gentiles "scientism," were it not for the fact that all scientists do not hold it. The other name that is currently available is "positivism" and we shall use that without distinction among subordinate kinds [22]. As we shall presently see, it is a fact of no slight significance that those who have expounded the position of positivism have, at all times, regarded themselves as, in some sense of the word, "philosophers."

I turn now to a statement of the differences between the 13th-century situation in theology and the present one in philosophy. The differences naturally follow from the distinction between the spheres of faith and reason [23]. In the first place, St. Thomas could argue on philosophical grounds that truths of faith and truths of reason either cover common ground or, not concurring in this way, are nevertheless compatible [24]. Winning this point, he could proceed to establish philosophical truths as preambles to faith in so far as there was concurrence. In the second place, he could offer philosophical arguments in probable support of faith in matters entirely exceeding reason,—the mysteries of theology; or at least could resolve objections brought on philosophical grounds by showing the errors they contained [25]. How different is our situation! For by the very fact that our adversaries deny that philosophy is knowledge in the sense we claim, we are necessarily precluded from using philosophical arguments of any sort to show the distinction, the independence, and the harmony of philosophy and science. To do so would be to beg the whole question and that is precisely what we have so often been charged with doing. Furthermore, although we willingly assent to all the well-tested conclusions of science, there are no scientific propositions which, strictly speaking, are preambles to philosophy as the philosophical truth that God exists or that the soul is immortal is a preamble to faith. Finally, we are prevented from answering objections by what we hold to be sound philosophical arguments for the same reason that we cannot use these arguments to establish the existence of philosophical knowledge in the first place. Let me make this last point clear. The problem of the nature and the kinds of knowledge is, from our point of view, a philosophical problem which can be truly solved. But to solve it requires propositions from several philosophical subject-matters: metaphysics, the philosophy of nature, and psychology. In short, we can proceed demonstratively only by affirming a large number of philosophical truths. And our right to do so is precisely what is challenged.

Strange as it may seem, the task of the philosopher *contra* positivists appears to be much more difficult than that of a Christian theologian addressing Moors on questions of faith. Yet it is not impossible so long as our adversaries will find self-contradiction repugnant. We can at least "have recourse to natural reason, to which all are compelled to assent" [26]. In this respect, positivists are not beyond the pale, as are those skeptics who are not even silenced by their own contradictions. We learn from St. Thomas that, in matters where faith proposes what exceeds reason's demonstrative power, "our intention must be not to convince our opponent by our arguments, but to solve the arguments which he brings against the truth" [27]. And, to paraphrase another passage, if our opponent agrees to no philosophical truth, there is no longer any means of proving any part of such truth by reasoning, but only of answering his objections. Since the contrary of a truth can never be demonstrated, it is clear that the arguments brought against the truths of philosophy cannot be demonstrations, but are difficulties which can be answered [28]. This is, of course, a purely negative procedure, but have we tried it as fully as St. Thomas did in answering the objections of the gentiles? Have we not almost always strayed into the easier path of demonstrating the errors of the positivists, easier but totally ineffective since demonstration must be from principles which, according to them, beg the question? The work I am proposing is both wearisome and exacting. It will require us to state the objections of our opponents as fairly and fully as St. Thomas did in the *Summa Contra Gentiles* [29]. We must master, for instance, all the technical innovations of the logical positivists, in order to state their arguments in a manner familiar to them. But is not the prize worthy of the effort? For if this issue can be resolved, the way is clear for the progressive resolution of other issues, even to the most momentous conclusions of metaphysics and natural theology. Failing here, we may possess the truth and meditate upon it, but we cannot perform the other duties of the wise man: to disseminate it and free it from error.

It remains to ask whether there is any positive course we can pursue. If we turn again to our 13th-century analogue, we must guard against a too easy transposition. The relation of scientific knowledge to philosophy is not the same as the relation of philosophical knowledge to sacred doctrine [30]. Nevertheless, I venture to suggest a number of respects in which we can begin by accepting some part of our opponent's position and proceed positively to our own. In the first place, the very existence of science itself can serve as a preamble to philosophy, and this in a number of ways: *first,* in that those who affirm the conclusions of science to be knowledge of an independent real are themselves uttering a philosophical proposition, since this proposition is clearly not itself a conclusion of any of the investigative sciences; *second,* in that whatever account is given of the truth of scientific knowledge, a distinction is necessarily made between knower and known which leads to a discussion of modes of being, in what manner knowledge exists in contrast to that which is known; *third,* in that science is useful practically in directing operations performed upon physical things, yet it does not provide us with the knowledge to determine whether this or that operation should be performed; *fourth,* in that science employs certain propositions in the interpretation of its data, which the scientist does not himself establish and which, therefore, the scientist regards as assumptions he must make, but which may cease to be assumptions when carried to their ultimate grounds. In all this, it will be helpful to point out that the positivist who discusses such matters does so not in the capacity of an investigator in some department of natural or social science, but rather as a "philosopher," by which he means a grammarian or a logician. We can proceed, further, therefore, by inquiring concerning the kind of knowledge which the grammarian and the logician have. It is admittedly not science of the real, for science itself is its object of knowledge. This admission carries with it, not only the distinction between different kinds of knowledge, but that there can be a true and a false, or at least a better and worse, account of the nature of science itself. From this point it should not be difficult to show that our opponents have a theory of knowledge which includes many philosophical propositions that cannot be reduced to the postulates of syntax or the rules of logistic [31].

In the second place, the limitations of science provide a preamble to philosophy, and this in two ways: *first,* intrinsically, from the account given by the positivists of the nature of science as extending only to that which is directly sensible or discoverable by sensitive instruments, for this account does not prove what they maintain, i.e., the impossibility of knowledge proceeding from the sensible to the intelligible; nor can such an impossibility be shown without entering into a discussion which is itself philosophical in a way that exceeds the spheres of grammar and logic; *second,* extrinsically, from the fact, admitted by all, that science has a history and that the history of science is knowledge about science, both different from science itself and from the account which the positivists give of the nature of science. The existence of historical knowledge shows that science is not the only knowledge of the real, and from the fact that man can know the real in at least two diverse ways follows the probability, at least, that there are still other modes of knowing, of which philosophy may be one. Further, it is generally admitted that history does not supplant science, nor science history, and that changes in the one sort of knowledge do not necessarily require changes in the other; from which it is arguable that there is a certain independence between bodies of knowledge of essentially diverse sorts, so that if philosophy is a third sort of knowledge, it too may be thus independent of the others. Finally, the history of science shows how, in some respects, scientific research corrects erroneous opinions held by men, whereas in others it merely confirms what men commonly knew without research of any sort. If we can enumerate these matters of common knowledge to the satisfaction of our adversaries, we shall possess the only basis in fact needed to establish, in a thoroughly *a posteriori* fashion, propositions in the philosophy of nature compatible at every point with scientific knowledge [32]. In proceeding thus it would be well to emphasize that if there are many different sorts of knowledge about the world, each has limitations appropriate to its nature, and that whereas we have used the limitations of science to show the possibility of philosophy, we can use the limitations of philosophy to show the necessity of science [33]. Furthermore, the continuity of science, which is technical knowledge, with the knowledge men commonly possess without any special technique should enable us to explicate a similar continuity in the case of technical philosophy. This will require us to distinguish the techniques, but in such a way that the positivist will see that all knowledge, technical or otherwise, is from experience, is verified in experience, and is subject to the same formal conditions of grammar and logic.

In the third place, supposing the foregoing steps to have been taken, we can proceed to present the philosophy of nature as a body of knowledge to be examined in the light of all the strictures positivists may wish to impose. This should be done not only for the purpose of satisfying all criteria of verification, but more significantly in order to show that since this knowledge is verified directly in experience, it depends in no way upon the changing content of science. This, further, will enable us to demonstrate as philosophically true those basic principles of method and interpretation which all scientists find it necessary to assume. If we propose any propositions which are not required by and verifiable in experience, which are not consistent with science, or which depend logically upon scientific findings, our opponents should be able to correct us on these points and require us to withdraw our claims. Failing to do so, they must admit our case.

There is one point that I wish to stress here. We customarily think of metaphysics as the first philosophy. We talk a great deal about proceeding from first principles. But we also know that the order of exposition is not the order of learning, that the order of demonstration is not the dialectical way. If we are teaching dialectically we must proceed in the order of learning, which is to begin with the most obvious facts attested by every man's experience and come gradually by patient analysis to the terms required if what every one knows is to be rendered intelligible.

Our procedure must be entirely inductive, thoroughly *a posteriori* [34]. Engaged as we are in an ascending dialectic, the philosophy of nature comes first and the first principles of metaphysics come last. Although we know that the philosophy of nature presupposes certain metaphysical concepts, it is advisable to use these as if they were part of the natural equipment of any intelligent man [35]. If we can restrain ourselves from exhibitions of technical expertness, we may be able to divest metaphysics of its horrors and have our positivist friends talking metaphysics without knowing it. We shall have removed the stumbling block. For St. Thomas, natural theology was the bridge between philosophy and faith. For us the philosophy of nature, the analysis of change in the phenomenal world which science investigates, must be the stepping stone from the natural sciences to metaphysics in its fullness, including natural theology [36].

In all this I have barely sketched and vaguely suggested the outline of a contemporary *Contra Gentiles.* I hope I have done enough to indicate plainly that the way is long and hard. I feel sure that he who does not find it so is not taking the way which leads the gentiles to philosophy. Unfortunately, there are even further things to do if we are willing to face all the issues which the modern world presents. I turn, therefore, to a brief consideration of these further problems.

III.

You will recall that St. Thomas distinguished Mohammedans and other pagans from Jews, and both of these as infidels from heretics. It was necessary to do so, for the conditions of argument in each of these three cases were different [37]. The *Summa Contra Gentiles* regarded all three adversaries in its exposition and defense of the Christian faith; but always bearing the important distinctions in mind. So far we have considered only one sort of gentile from the point of view of philosophical truth, the positivist who is the analogue of the Moor. Can the analogy be safely carried further to include those whose relations to philosophy are as the positions of the Jew and heretic were to Christian dogma? I think it can, if we remember all the necessary qualifications in making the transposition. Thus, like the Jew in matters of religion, there is in the modern world the philosopher who, while agreeing that philosophy is knowledge having a validity independent of science, insists upon an irreducible plurality of philosophies, each of them true according to the postulates from which they arise. And, like the Christian heretic, there is the philosopher who, while agreeing that there is only one true philosophy, differs from us in this or that particular.

There is not time to sketch, even as inadequately as in the case of the positivist, the procedure by which we must engage in these two further fields of modern controversy. It will be agreed, however, that our work cannot stop short of the full task. And it will be seen, I hope, that failure to deal separately with each of these three sorts of gentiles must result in an exasperating confusion of issues. I have long suspected that much contemporary polemic is baffling because of this fact. St. Thomas proposed an order of topics which was fitting for the exposition of faith to the gentiles [38]. That cannot be our order, obviously, because of the difference of our sphere; but there is an order which the nature of the case imposes upon us: first, to argue with the positivists that philosophy is knowledge; second, and only then, to argue with the systematists that there is only one body of philosophical knowledge; and third, to argue with differing philosophers about the truth of particular propositions [39].

In the time that is left, I can do no more than make tangential comments on the systematists, and on the heretics within philosophy itself.

I have used the name "systematist" to designate those who hold to an irreducible plurality of philosophies, because they conceive of a philosophy as if it were like a mathematical system, such as a system of geometry. In the same way that mathematical systems are multiplied by the choice of different initial postulates and definitions,—as, for instance, the various non-Euclidean geometries,—diverse systems of philosophy are generated by arbitrarily made assumptions and definitions. The choice of the postulates is determined by the kind of system one wishes to develop [40]. The truth of the system is measured by its deductive coherence, the inner consistency of all its propositions. It is difficult to say in what sense different systems of mathematics have a common subject-matter, but it is generally supposed that they do not contradict each other. Their multiplicity expresses the fecundity of the mathematical imagination, its logical fertility in the construction of systems. Since those who take this view rarely if ever consider mathematics to be knowledge of the world of actual existences, they are left free to play in their make-believe world of intellectual toys. The law of contradiction does not enter there except as a rule of operation in system development. It applies within systems, but not between systems. It does not seem to require obedience to a reality which can be rightly described in one way and one way only.

To refute the systematist in philosophy it is necessary to show him that he has been misled by his analogy of philosophy with mathematics [41]. He must assert either that philosophy is the same as mathematics in its subject-matter and methods,—holding in this case that it is not knowledge of the real,—or that philosophy differs from mathematics in both of these respects. If he take the first horn of the dilemma, his position is essentially the same as that of the positivist, and we have no further problem with him; if he take the second, he must hold that philosophy, unlike mathematics in his view of it, and like the natural sciences, is knowledge of the real world. Once he has granted this much, it will be possible to show him, by many steps of argument, first, that if there were two systems of philosophy both could not be true, and second, that there cannot be two systems of philosophy because not even one is possible.

On the first count, supposing there were two comprehensive systems of philosophy, they must either have the same subject-matter, or not. Only if not, could conflict between them be avoided; but it would be impossible for two systems to be *comprehensive* accounts of the *real world* and not have common subject-matter. Since, then, they must have the same subject-matter,—which means that they offer us knowledge concerning the same formal object,—the criteria by which either one can be judged true make it inevitable that the other one be regarded as false. But which is true, it may still be asked; and the systematist may still try to answer that either one may be true, and the other false, according as you arbitrarily choose these postulates and definitions or those. Now either this is a purely verbal point he is making,—the systems differing grammatically as two languages, or rhetorically as two speeches, saying the same thing,—or he is trying to maintain what is impossible logically, namely, that different premises and definitions can alternatively demonstrate the truth of contradictory conclusions without being affected themselves. For if the falsity of a conclusion reflects upon its premises, the choice between truth and falsity is inevitable with respect to the premises as well as the conclusions. It cannot be held, therefore, that the method of postulates avoids the issue.

With this we proceed to the second count, which goes to the root of the matter. The philosopher makes no postulates because he does not construct a system in any proper sense analogous to the structure of a geometry [42]. If the word "deduction" be used to describe the procession of theorems in the order of a mathematical system, then it must be said that philosophy is not deductive. The order of philosophical demonstration is much more like that of the empirical sciences. It is inductive and *a posteriori* in the sense that it begins with observable facts and proceeds by various steps to *explain* them, to render them intelligible, just as the scientist proceeds from his data to formulate accurate *descriptions* of the phenomena. A philosopher claims to demonstrate his conclusion only when he is able to show that it alone, of an exhaustive set of alternatives, is compatible with all the facts and explanatory of them. It would, thus, appear that the philosopher like the scientist uses the method of multiple working hypotheses; but there is this difference: that the philosopher can make an exhaustive enumeration of hypotheses and, therefore, determine without contingency the right choice to be made. The body of philosophical knowledge, as a whole or divided into its component subject-matters, is no more a system-structure than the body of the natural sciences, if the latter be separated from the mathematics it often includes. "The three greatest metaphysicians who ever existed," Gilson concludes, "had no system in the idealistic sense of the word. Their ambition was not to achieve philosophy once and for all, but to maintain it and to serve it in their own times, as we have to maintain it and to serve it in ours" [43].

May I add that Thomists have not been without fault in this respect. Unless they correct their own careless references to the philosophy of St. Thomas as a great *system* of thought, as a magnificent avalanche of syllogisms falling in an orderly cascade from first principles, they cannot object to aesthetic comparisons of Thomism with the other systems of philosophy our culture so richly affords. Yet they should object most strenuously because they should renounce even the name "Thomism" if it tends to signify a system of philosophy in any sense that suggests a justifiable plurality of points of view in philosophy. They should even protest against the praise which the gentiles so willingly bestow upon the work of St. Thomas as a great piece of intellectual architecture because this, too, carries the imputation of "the mediaeval synthesis," a system flawlessly constructed but serviceable, of course, only in its own time, except as a monument to be admired. We cannot understand what *philosophia perennis* means unless we are willing to abjure every *ism* which connotes a personal system of thought for, as Gilson points out, that name is not "an honorary title for any particular form of philosophical thinking, but a necessary designation for philosophy itself, almost a tautology. That which is philosophical,"—but not *a* philosophy,—"is perennial in its own right" [44].

I would go further and suggest making a number of acknowledgments to clarify our position against the systematists. First, let us admit that when we speak of first principles in philosophy, we mean what the modern world calls tautologies. This will make perfectly plain that our first principles are not postulates, because there is no need to assume a tautology. They are tautologies in the sense that as immediate or self-evident propositions they do no more than explicate the intentions of our concepts. Their truth is seen immediately upon the understanding of the terms which compose them. We differ from our contemporaries who dismiss tautologies as verbalisms, not by avoiding tautologies, but by seeing that they add to the knowledge which is contained in our concepts if only by a step of explication. We do not know more through them, but what we know we know more explicitly [45].

Then, let us repudiate the notion of systematic deduction by showing that the *Summa Theologica,* for instance, far from being the perfection of linear inference, is essentially circular in its intellectual movement. The vast series of questions is clearly ordered, of course, but the ordering is in terms of whole problems and parts and not in terms of an asymmetrical relation of premises and conclusions. St. Thomas employs propositions in earlier questions which must wait many pages, often many books, before their own truth is made clear. And the truth of the earlier conclusions cannot be fully understood until much that follows is gone through. The movement of thought is in an ever widening series of concentric circles. This is not deduction in the mathematical sense, but enlightenment in the philosophical sense. We are more concerned with making our understanding sure than with a superficial progression of demonstrations. I would almost say that the essential logic of philosophical thought is circular, and mean by that to speak its praise by comparison with the extremely discursive character of mathematics. To say this is not to admit the fallacy of *in circulo probando,* any more than to admit the tautology of all indemonstrable truths is to say that they are not genuinely knowledge. Both tautology and circularity are signs that philosophical reasoning more nearly approaches intellection in its mode of knowing, and in this it is superior to mathematics and the sciences which, as more discursive, approach the imagination and the senses. The philosopher, being human and hence unable to grasp the whole area of the intelligible in a single act, approximates this by a radial motion circumscribing the point to be known [46]. Mathematics and the sciences move on from one thing to another. It is their logic, not that of philosophy, which the ordinary text-books describe [47].

Finally, let us disclaim the flawlessness of St. Thomas if thereby is attributed to his work complete freedom from contradictions. The *Summa Theologica* answers its many questions by the resolution of contradictory positions, the reconciliation of extremes which have some common ground. By the repeated distinction between what is said *simpliciter* and what is said *secundum quid,* and similar techniques, St. Thomas is able to assimilate all the truth that contrary errors seem to contain. But the process is necessarily limited because the human understanding is naturally limited. At crucial points contradictions or apparent oppositions are left unresolved. Let us not try to conceal or even eliminate these crucial flaws because they are precious to the integrity of philosophy as signs of its self-discipline, its recognition of philosophical mysteries which mark the boundaries of our unaided understanding. If, again, the modern world has an invidious name for the unresolved contradiction, let us not cringe before the word "antinomy," but praise St. Thomas for discerning the basic antinomies of philosophical thought, many centuries before Kant's less successful effort. Just as in the case of tautology and circularity, antinomy can be regarded as a proper mark of philosophy. There are, strictly speaking, no antinomies in empirical science. But here as before, the dyslogistic sense of the word must be corrected. The antinomy points to a mystery, to something which escapes our understanding not through being unintelligible in itself but because its intelligibility exceeds our power of knowing [48].

There are two errors to be avoided here. One is the notion, prevalent among systematists, that one system of philosophy is about as good as another because all of them sooner or later end in antinomies. What should be said is that one philosopher is better than another in proportion as he does not try speciously to avoid antinomies at the places where they should occur and does not get involved in contradictions which are due not to the essential limitations of the human mind but to his own peculiar errors. The other mistake to be avoided is the supposition that an antinomy invalidates the analysis from which it issues. If that were the case, there would be no philosophical truth at all. But it is not the case. The mistake here comes from confusing the antinomy, following from an analysis, with a false proposition following from premises in linear inference. The latter does invalidate its sources, but the antinomy protects the analysis it concludes from exceeding the bounds of reason. If it is truly an antinomy it confirms the analysis as having been carried to its limit [49].

We can now turn to the last part of our modern *Contra Gentiles.* The points which have been made in dealing with the positivist and the systematist will facilitate our treatment of the last of the gentiles, the heretic in philosophy. The root of all philosophical error is the failure upon the part of thinkers to be philosophers in method and subject-matter. Thus, the positivist tries to reduce philosophy to the empirical sciences or to restrict it to grammar and logic; the systematist is given to mathematizing philosophy and this leads to further transgressions of subject-matter. There are still other similar sources of error: exclusive emphasis upon physics or psychology; the confusion of philosophy with, or its subjection to, theology [50]. A proper development of the philosophy of nature can protect us from all misdirections and wrong emphases except the last; it will discriminate the truly physical from mathematical questions; and it will determine the lower limits of philosophical knowledge by indicating the questions which the philosopher cannot, and therefore must not, answer [51]. These must forever remain open for scientific investigation. But the upper limit of philosophy,—the line which divides its domain from that of dogmatic theology,—can be determined only in two ways: either by the self-discipline of the philosopher, critical of reason's powers and sensitive to the mysteries which terminate metaphysical inquiry, or by the guidance afforded the philosopher by faith [52]. Either of these two means alone is likely to miscarry. Without the restrictions imposed by sacred doctrine, the metaphysician is always in danger of going too far. Without the self-discipline of philosophical criticism, dogmatic theology can become constitutive of philosophical answers, instead of being merely regulative of its sphere of questions. The great virtue of St. Thomas as a philosopher was that he perfectly combined the theologian with the philosopher. Never confusing the two domains, his reason could lead to faith and his faith seek understanding without disorder or imbalance. There is no modern, not even Kant, who exemplifies better the critical spirit of philosophy itself, and there are many who indulge in gnosticism, who confuse theology and philosophy, who rashly submit to reason questions which can be answered only by faith [53].

Although it will be the longest part of our *Contra Gentiles,*—since its scope will include the major questions of philosophy,—this part devoted to the correction of philosophical error will be by far the easiest. The reason is simple. Here we can get the most help from St. Thomas. He did not face positivism and systematism in their distinctive modern forms. To combat these tendencies, therefore, requires dialectical ingenuity, as well as new knowledge, on our part. But there are no peculiarly modern heresies within the province of philosophy itself. That all the errors which have occurred in modern philosophy repeat the falsities of ancient and mediaeval thought is, perhaps, the most striking sign of the perennial character of philosophical truth [54]. There is nothing strictly new about modern materialism or idealism, empiricism or rationalism, naturalism or absolutism. For each of these errors an ancient or mediaeval thinker could be named to parallel his modern counterpart, often superior to the latter in the lucidity of his deviation from the truth. All of these *isms* are to be understood as extremes, containing some truth, but false through failure to possess the truth which is also contained in the opposite extreme [55]. The whole truth lies between them in the eminent mean which is a synthesis of, not a compromise between, their partial, hence inadequate, insights. To attain this whole truth is obviously the work of intellectual virtue; the extremes of speculative vice are in every case either an excess, which is dogmatism, or a defect, which is agnosticism [56]. We can best praise the philosophy of St. Thomas as exhibiting the almost perfect speculative prudence which enabled him to achieve so much truth, not merely by avoiding so many errors but by salvaging from the extremes all that could be embraced in moderation and thus rectified [57].

In imitating the work of St. Thomas,—which is our only right to call ourselves Thomists,—we must strive to remove one misapprehension of our efforts, for which we are partly responsible. We too frequently speak in the negative, or so, at least, we permit ourselves to be understood. We are regarded as dismissing the whole of modern philosophy as a vortex of errors. We are supposed to hold that St. Thomas possessed all speculative truth, which it is our duty to regain by a sort of nostalgic return. These misconceptions arise in part from our rightful insistence upon the quantity of truth which St. Thomas provides us with as a starting point, as well as from our claim, also justified, that he corrected errors and solved difficulties which have recurred since his day. But it is a starting point, and not the whole truth, for there is obviously work to be done. And if ancient errors have reappeared in modern thought, so has ancient truth. Therefore, we should be able to avoid these misconceptions in so far as they follow from our manner of speech or undue emphasis upon what is to be rejected rather than saved.

The highest praise that can be paid the 13th-century achievement of St. Thomas turns not merely on the errors he criticized and the truth he reclaimed by their correction, but more positively upon the point that he could embrace all the truth of antiquity. "Because he had the utmost reverence for the doctors of antiquity," Cajetan says, "he seems to have inherited in a way the intellect of all" [58]. He more accurately speaks Plato's mind than Plato, more explicitly expresses Aristotle than Aristotle. If the traditions of Platonism and Aristotelianism appear to be in opposition, it is because neither Plato nor Aristotle grasped the truth of the other and hence did not understand themselves as well as St. Thomas understands them [59]. In the hands of most of their followers, their partial truths are debased to the contrary errors of Platonism and Aristotelianism. But St. Thomas was not an ordinary follower. He was a philosopher, not a scholiast, and his abundant genius penetrated the texts of Plato and Aristotle to the complementary truths they intended. It did not stop at the verbal surface where they often appear irreconcilable [60].

If we praise St. Thomas in this way, we must try to imitate him accordingly. I can barely suggest to you what that means for the part of our work which should assimilate the truths of modern thought. But a few points are clear in the light of St. Thomas's teaching. We must combine the *a posteriori* method of proceeding always from experience, which is the great virtue of Locke's contribution, with the self-critical yet constructive exercise of reason, which modern thought owes to Kant [61]. If we unite these two essential conditions of philosophic method, we should be able to produce a synthesis of Hume's insight concerning problems in the phenomenal order with the vision of Leibnitz about the intelligible world of being. We should be able to do, in short, what Kant himself tried to do, but did not do well enough, as the historical consequences make plain [62]. I have mentioned only the outstanding contributions of modern thought, in terms of its problems, its insights, its efforts. But that is enough to indicate how a modern *Contra Gentiles,* a philosophical summa, could be not just polemically negative but positively synthetic, presenting the philosophy of nature and metaphysics in so clear a light that modern times would be able to see the best image of its thought reflected therein. Even epistemology might be subdued to its proper place and in a theory of knowledge which derived from metaphysics rather than destroyed it, the account of vision as the goal toward which all human knowledge and discursive reason tend would include the positive note in the Hegelian yearning for the Absolute. But, with William James, we know that the world is a vast plurality of finite things, yet not, therefore, irrational, illusory or self-contradictory;

the vision of the One comes only after we have reasoned and lived our way through this concatenated universe of the contingent many [63].

IV.

The conclusion with which this discussion must end is only too obvious. It is easier to praise St. Thomas than to imitate him. The project I have vaguely envisaged would require genius to accomplish, and perhaps even more than genius in the way of moral and intellectual gifts. For speculative prudence alone is not sufficient for the operations of intellectual virtue whereby a large sum of truth is known. Courage also is needed; without it, the docility which is a part of prudence may become mere indolence. So, too, temperance is necessary, for he who is too aggressive in the pursuit of his object, even truth, may rashly overreach his abilities. It is the right proportion of these parts which makes for genius in any human work, and genius itself may be wayward and intermittent unless fortified by grace [64]. Most of us know our rank among men too well to rush in where only the angelic doctor need not fear to tread.

Yet if we have talents to use, there must

be a task befitting our station. Though St. Thomas was the wise master who planned well and executed much, materials were prepared for him by the labors of many men, some now anonymous, some favored by memory. There is enough labor of this sort for all of us to do, who share the dream of philosophy reaching its modern maturity. The right way to anticipate the genius needed to fulfill our hope is to prepare the way for him. Anything else would be day-dreaming. We shall be good followers of St. Thomas through working for the future, not through looking to the past.

There are many things, of course, which might appear to justify a man in calling himself a Thomist [65]. He might spend his life among the texts trying to purify them of their minor aberrancies by collating passages, or seeking to resolve their major antinomies. I cannot commend either of these occupations to you as philosophers. The former is scholarship or, worse, system-building, and the latter partakes of *hybris,* proudly unmindful of the limits of reason. Or a man might devote himself to teaching, by spoken or written word, the philosophy he has learned from St. Thomas. This is work which must be done and to do it well is both honorable and in the service of philosophy. But I reserve the highest commendation for a third undertaking. It is to engage in the labors I have described [66]. It is to perform the dialectical tasks by which philosophy is kept alive. The man who performs them, however slight his contribution to the ultimate whole, is more fully alive, more actually a philosopher, than any other. If Thomism is not a school of philosophy, not one philosophy among many, if the philosophy of St. Thomas is simply philosophy itself, living perennially today as in the 13th century, then the man who participates in it by dialectical efforts worthy of its goal should signalize his devotion to St. Thomas by regarding himself, not as a Thomist, but simply as a philosopher. Thus he would call himself by a name common to all who have the same vocation, the love and service of truth. Should the world be fortunate enough to have another St. Thomas appear, he more than any other would rightly be called a philosopher and not a Thomist. I say this in the spirit of St. Thomas, the spirit in which he left his own work incomplete and placed philosophy itself below other things in the scale of goods. For wisdom is greater than the men who love it, and therefore the proper name of no man can be used to circumscribe the truth.

NOTES

1. St. Thomas frequently employs the Aristotelian precept: quod non potest effici per unum, fiat aliqualiter per plura. Thus, "As the Philosopher says (*De Caelo,* ii, 12), the lowest order of things cannot acquire perfect goodness, but they acquire a certain imperfect goodness, by a few movements; and those which belong to a higher order acquire perfect goodness by many movements; and those yet higher acquire perfect goodness by few movements; and the highest perfection is found in those things which acquire perfect goodness without any movement whatever" (*Summa Theologica,* I,Q.77,A.2). Cf. *Summa Theologica,* I-II,Q.5, A.7. This applies to the perfection of knowledge as well as to the perfection of being. Man's cognitive limitations are indicated by the multiple operations of sense and reason by which he knows. This is indicated in another way by the fact that man does not know nature by one kind of knowledge, but by many, such as history, the arts, science, and philosophy. Vd. P. Rousselot, *The Intellectualism of St. Thomas,* New York, 1935: Ch. III and IV. Cf. T. Gilbey, *Poetic Experience,* New York, 1934.

2. "It is the function of the wise man to put things in order, because wisdom is primarily the perfection of reason and it is the characteristic of reason to know order" (St. Thomas, *In Eth.,* lect. 1). Cf. *Summa Contra Gentiles,* I, 1. And Gilson's comment on the role of St. Thomas in the mediae-

val experiment is relevant here: "While so many men were trying to base philosophy on theological foundations, a very simple and modest man was putting everything in its place. His name was Thomas Aquinas. . . . Himself a theologian, St. Thomas had asked the professors of theology never to prove an article of faith by rational demonstration. . . . He had likewise asked the professors of philosophy never to prove a philosophical truth by resorting to the words of God. . . . These two sciences are bound ultimately to agree; but if you really want them to agree, you must first be careful not to forget their essential difference. Only distinct things can be united; if you attempt to blend them, you inevitably lose them in what is not union, but confusion" (*Unity of Philosophical Experience,* New York, 1937: pp. 61-62).

3. To the question, whether the Church has canonized the philosophy of St. Thomas, in the sense of imposing it in virtue of her doctrinal magistracy, Maritain answers: "No doctrine of purely human wisdom could possibly be described, in strictness of terms, as 'the Catholic philosophy.' There can be no 'philosophical system which a man must adopt in order to be a Christian' (Sertillanges). . . . A philosophy is not imposed upon the mind by means of authority; to do so would be a defiance of the very nature of things, philosophy being essentially the work of reason" (*St. Thomas Aquinas,* London, 1933: pp. 168-169).

Cf. *ibid.,* pp. 124-126. In matters of science, St. Thomas had clearly said, "The argument from authority based on human reason is the weakest" (*Summa Theologica,* I,Q.1,A.8,ad.2). The association of the name of St. Thomas with the notion of undue authoritarianism in the realm of reason is fantastic. It can be accounted for only by a lack of proper docility on the part of those who make the charge. Vd. Maritain, *op. cit.,* pp. 92-93.

4. "St. Thomas Aquinas as a Philosopher" in *Philosophical Studies,* London: 1934. Vd. esp. pp. 226, 247, 250-253, 256-257.

5. "Thomist philosophy is no mere Aristotelianism revised but a masterly synthesis of both Plato and Aristotle with one another and with St. Augustine" (A. E. Taylor, *op. cit.,* p. 247). "By comparison with the Thomist synthesis of Plato, Aristotle, and Augustine, how comparatively incoherent and loose is Kant's synthesis of Hume and Leibniz" (*Ibid.,* p. 253).

6. *The Spirit of Mediaeval Philosophy,* New York, 1936: Ch. I, II. Cf. Gilson, *Christianisme et Philosophie,* Paris, 1936; and Maritain, *De La Philosophie Chrétienne,* Paris, 1933.

7. *The Unity of Philosophical Experience,* New York, 1937: pp. 318-319. "The history of philosophy is to the philosopher what his laboratory is to the scientist; it particularly shows how philosophers do not think as they wish, but as they can, for the interrelation of philosophical ideas is just

as independent of us as are the laws of the physical world" (*Ibid.*, p. 120). Cf. Professor Cohen: "The history of philosophy (is) a laboratory of intellectual experiments, where we may learn from past thinkers by observing the results of their experiments" (Phil. Rev., 39, 2: p. 132). We may wonder with Gilson, though, how many "experiments will be necessary before men acquire some philosophical experience" (*Op. cit.*, p. 59).

8. *New York Times Book Review,* Jan. 30, 1938: p. 4.

9. *The Nation,* Feb. 19, 1938: pp. 219-220. "In spite of his extraordinary erudition M. Gilson permits his dogmatism to betray him. And yet the error into which it leads him is not difficult to demonstrate. . . . Is it not rather easy to show that Plato and Aristotle committed the very same error of which the philosophers who are said to have failed are accused. And if Aristotle, then Thomas. For Plato's thought borrowed its orientation from his interest in geometry. And Aristotle attempted to correct his teacher's errors by means of a poor biology and a physics at least as poor—both poor because verbal. And if Thomas was not guided by a positive science of which he was a master by right of his own contributions to it, it was simply because the best science within his reach was that of Aristotle. Thus the perennial philosophy to which M. Gilson would bring us back is a philosophy grounded on an inadequate science twenty-five hundred years old."

10. "A sound philosophy can therefore dispense with the particular system of scientific explanations of which it makes use in accordance with the state of science at a particular epoch, and if that system were one day proved false, the truth of that philosophy would not be affected. Only its language and the sensible illustrations with which it clothed its truths would require modifications. . . . The purely scientific mistakes to be found in older statements of Aristotelian and Thomistic philosophy, statements which inevitably bear the stamp of the scientific beliefs of their period, do nothing to discredit the truth of that philosophy" (Maritain, *Introduction to Philosophy,* New York, 1930: pp. 120-121). And in a footnote, he adds: "The 'crime' of the decadent scholastics of the 16th and 17th centuries was that they believed, and made others believe, that the philosophy of Aristotle and St. Thomas was bound up with the mistakes of ancient science, of which it is in reality wholly independent" (*Ibid.,* p. 122).

Cf. *Les Degrés du Savoir,* Paris, 1932: Ch. 2, esp. pp. 100-102, 118-119. On the relations of natural science to natural philosophy, vd. *La Philosophie de la Nature,* Paris, 1935. On the difference between progress in scientific knowledge and in philosophy, vd. *St. Thomas Aquinas*: pp. 13-14; *Theonas,* New York, 1933; and cf. Dr. Gerald Phelan, *Jacques Maritain,* New York, 1937: pp. 31 ff.

Cf. also A. D. Sertillanges, *St. Thomas Aquinas and His Work,* London, 1932: pp. 134-135. Sertillanges quotes St. Thomas as saying: "Any old woman today knows more about things divine than did all the philosophers of antiquity put together" (p. 46). Maritain's position can be expressed in the paraphrase: any college student today knows more science than all the mediaeval doctors. But the old woman was not a theologian, nor are our college students philosophers through their knowledge of science.

11. Thus, Gilson's reviewer in *The Nation* is contemptuous of his statement that Plato, Aristotle and St. Thomas looked "for an ultimate ground of all real and possible experience" under the guidance of "immutable principles." It is empty verbiage, according to the reviewer, to say that they found it "in the word 'Being,' spelled with a capital 'B'." So, too, "forms and potencies and entelechies explain nothing. Positive science explains very little indeed, but it does it well. Is it a wonder then that we prefer our unstable certainties to Thomas's and M. Gilson's immutable principles" (*loc. cit.*) In a similar vein, the leading philosopher of education in America today is charged with being a Thomist and, hence, unintelligible, because his discussion of *The Higher Learning in America* refers to metaphysics, first principles, and the study of being as being.

12. *St. Thomas Aquinas,* p. 15.

13. A. D. Sertillanges, *St. Thomas Aquinas and His Work,* p. 60. Cf. Maritain, *op. cit.,* p. 92: "*Doci-*

bilitas, the faculty of being taught, is an essential characteristic of the created mind. . . . Aristotle classifies animals according to that criterion, placing those that refuse to be taught on the lowest rung."

14. That I am hardly unaware of the difficulties can be gathered from remarks made by Dr. Alexander in his preface to my series of lectures *What Man Has Made of Man,* New York, 1937. Thus: "Scholasticism, a sterile form of deductive thinking, developed as a harmless outlet for the reasoning powers of man in a period of intellectual servitude when man could not observe the world around himself, lest any observation come in contradiction with prevailing dogma. He had to content himself with flawless deductions from incorrect premises. Free observation of facts was forbidden; rigid acceptance of preconceived ideas was the highest requisite of these mediaeval centuries" (*Op. cit.,* p. xvi).

15. Despite ample evidence to the contrary, I would still say that we should assume good will in those we seek to teach. Nor do I think making such an assumption is merely morally required in naive neglect of the facts, because I suspect the facts will show that many of those who reject our teaching, if they smell the faintest aroma of Thomism, do not do so from knowledge of St. Thomas's philosophy. They have not read him, nor tried to understand him; they have been prevented from doing so by an evil rumor of what Thomism is,

spread by the malicious or caused by our own poor rhetoric. How can we tell what the disposition of their will would be if we could remove these obstacles to their docility? Wherever the fault lies, the rumor of Thomism has scandalized many. Our task is not only to disseminate the truth, but to avoid scandal in doing so. Vd. *Summa Theologica,* II-II, Q.10,A.11, and elsewhere.

16. I am not certain that the policy I am here recommending is the same as the programme outlined by leaders of the Thomistic revival. Cf. Maritain, *St. Thomas Aquinas,* pp. 79, 107-109, 110-112, 174-175; A. D. Sertillanges, *op. cit.,* 127-150. Thus, Sertillanges calls for the production of a new Summa, "summarizing contemporary thought, as St Thomas's *Summa* summarized the thought of the past" (p. 149). This does not decide what seems to me the crucial question: which Summa? The *Summa Contra Gentiles* or the *Summa Theologica?* It is important which of these is placed first in the order of work to be done.

17. *Summa Contra Gentiles,* I, 1.

18. The discrimination of Mohammedan, Jew, and heretic must be made "because some of them, like the Mohammedans and pagans, do not agree with us as to the authority of any Scripture whereby they may be convinced, in the same way as we are able to dispute with the Jews by means of the Old Testament, and with heretics by means of the

New: whereas the former accept neither" (*Summa Contra Gentiles,* I, 2). Cf. *Summa Theologica,* I, Q.1, A.8: "We can argue with heretics from texts in Holy Writ, and against those who deny one article of faith we can argue from another. If our opponent believes nothing of divine revelation, there is no longer any means of proving the articles of faith by reasoning, but only of answering his objections—if he has any—against faith."

19. Vd. my formulation of this issue in *What Man Has Made of Man,* New York, 1937: Lect. I. The case of mathematics requires special mention. The positivists make a distinction between real and formal sciences. The natural and social sciences, investigative in method, are sciences of the real. Mathematics, and with it logistic (the positivist's confusion of grammar and logic), are formal knowledge or, in some extreme views, are purely conventional. And "philosophy" is either logistic, i.e. formal science, or it is nonsense, a preposterous pretension to being knowledge of the real. Vd. R. Carnap, *Philosophy and Logical Syntax,* London, 1934; and *The Logical Syntax of Language,* New York, 1937.

20. Those who hold that philosophy is a kind of knowledge of the real which is, nevertheless, dependent on the contingent findings of the investigative sciences are, ultimately, reduced to viewing science and philosophy as continuous, not essentially different in kind, in their object or method. The difference becomes one of the degree of spec-

ulative generality in which the philosopher is permitted to indulge. Vd. A. N. Whitehead, *Process and Reality,* New York, 1929: Ch. I; and *Adventures of Ideas,* New York, 1933: Ch. IX.

21. In Part II of the Lecture only the first sort of philosophical gentile,—the analogue of the Moor in theology,—is being considered. The other two species of gentility are discussed in Part III.

22. Although positivism as a militantly anti-philosophical movement is currently identified with the work of the so-called logical positivists, represented by the work of Carnap, Reichenbach, Wittgenstein and others, the roots of positivism lie deep in European thought. Thus, Bertrand Russell as a logical empiricist stems from John Stuart Mill, and Mill from Comte and Hume. The essential position of positivism is shared by many who do not share the current devotion to logistic, such, for instance, as Dewey, the pragmatist, and Cassirer, the neo-Kantian. We can ignore the varieties of positivism because in all its forms it maintains the same major theses concerning the sphere of human knowledge. But we would do well to detect the earliest roots of positivism in such thinkers as Abelard,—who, like the contemporary Viennese, confused grammar and logic and made the amalgam equal the whole of philosophy,—and Ockham, who is certainly the forbear of Hume. Vd. Gilson, *The Unity of Philosophical Experience,* New York, 1937: pp. 17 ff., 64-68, 86-91. The advantage of going back to Ockham, for instance,

for a statement of positivism is that he was much more learned than our contemporaries and, indeed, a better dialectician. Through him as a stepping stone we should be able to make a more intelligent formulation of the objections to the Thomistic position than could readily be gathered directly from the writings of Russell or Carnap or Dewey.

23. The relation of philosophy and theology is not the same as the relation of science and philosophy. Both science and philosophy are natural knowledge, whereas theology, that is, dogmatic theology, derives from sacred scriptures, from revelation as a supernatural source of knowledge. Because "theology cannot develop in the human mind without making use of philosophical truths, which are established by reason" (Maritain, *St. Thomas Aquinas,* p. 131), theology as sacred doctrine is a philosophical explication of faith. But philosophy can develop independently of science. Science, therefore, is not a positive instrument used by the philosopher, as the theologian uses philosophy. Vd. Maritain, *Introduction to Philosophy,* Ch. VI, VII, esp. pp. 121 ff.; 129 ff.

24. "The existence of God and other like truths about God, which can be known by natural reason, are not articles of faith, but preambles to the articles; for faith presupposes natural knowledge, even as grace presupposes nature, and perfection supposes something that can be perfected. Nevertheless, there is nothing to prevent a man, who cannot grasp a proof, accepting, as a matter of

faith, something which in itself is capable of being scientifically known and demonstrated" (*Summa Theologica,* I,Q.2,A.2,ad.1). "In those things which we hold about God there is truth in two ways. For certain things that are true about God wholly surpass the capability of human reason, for instance that God is three and one; while there are certain things to which even natural reason can attain, for instance, that God is, that God is one, and others like these. . . . Accordingly some divine truths are attainable by human reason while others surpass the power of human reason" (*Summa Contra Gentiles,* I,3). Although there is some part of the truth of Christian faith which "surpasses the ability of human reason, nevertheless those things which are naturally instilled in human reason cannot be opposed to this truth. . . . Seeing that the false alone is opposed to the true, as evidently appears if we examine their definitions, it is impossible for the aforesaid truth of faith to be contrary to those principles which reason knows naturally. . . . From this we may evidently conclude that whatever arguments are alleged against the teachings of faith, they do not rightly proceed from the first self-evident principles instilled by nature" (*Ibid.,* I, 7). For further discussion of reason and faith, vd. *Summa Theologica,* II-II, Q.1,A.5,ad.4; Q.2,AA.4,10.

These, and related passages, state the position of St. Thomas against the Averroists who proposed the notion of a double truth, "by which the same thing may be true in philosophy, but false in theology" (Maritain, *Introduction to Philosophy,* p. 128). Cf. Maritain, *St. Thomas Aquinas,* p. 129; Rousselot, *op. cit.,* pp. 72-73; Sertillanges, *op. cit.,* pp. 38 ff.

25. "Human reason is adapted to the knowledge of the truth of faith, which can be known in the highest degree only by those who see the divine substance, in so far as it is able to put together certain probable arguments in support thereof, which nevertheless are insufficient to enable us to understand the aforesaid truth as though it were demonstrated to us or understood by us in itself. And yet, however weak these arguments may be, it is useful for the human mind to be practised therein, so long as it does not pride itself on having comprehended or demonstrated" (*Summa Contra Gentiles,* I, 8). Having distinguished those theological truths which are within reason's power from those which are purely matters of faith, exceeding reason, St. Thomas says that in regard to the first kind "we must proceed by demonstrative arguments whereby we can convince our adversaries. But since such arguments are not available in support of the second kind of truth, our intention must not be to convince our opponent by our arguments, but to solve the arguments which he brings against the truth, because, as shown above, natural reason cannot be opposed to the truth of faith" (*Summa Contra Gentiles,* I, 9). Cf. *Summa Theologica,* I,Q.1,A.8.

26. *Summa Contra Gentiles,* I,2.

27. *Summa Contra Gentiles,* I, 9. St. Thomas goes on to say that not even the probable arguments, which can "be adduced for the practise and help of the faithful," should be used for "the conviction of our opponents, because the very insufficiency of these arguments would rather confirm them in their error, if they thought that we assented to the truth of faith on account of such weak reasonings."

28. Cf. *Summa Theologica,* I,Q.1,A.8.

29. "Just as nobody can give a fair judgment without hearing the arguments for both sides, so he who studies philosophy judges the better, if he hears all the arguments of those who call it in question" (St. Thomas, *In Metaph.,* Lib. III, lect. 1). "The true philosopher, and *a fortiori* the saint," adds Sertillanges, "must take his stand beside his adversaries, not opposite them. He must collaborate: he must use their true statements, and even their errors, to elucidate the truth" (*Op. cit.,* p. 70). So little did St. Thomas fear opposition, "that he set himself up as his own opponent, and mustered the most formidable objections possible to his thesis. He puts forward the objections and the thesis with the same calmness, however sacred the subject, and appears to bestow the same care on each. It is extraordinary to see the calm way this saint sets snares for God, siding with atheists, agnostics, heretics and pagans, more strongly than the most rabid unbelievers" (*Ibid.,* pp. 71-72). There is obviously a lesson in this for us if we

would accomplish a contemporary *Contra Gentiles*. We must formulate better objections than can be found in the writings of our adversaries, who really do not know our position well enough to object clearly and cogently. Vd. Note 22 *supra*.

30. The point here is simply that science is not an apologetical instrument for philosophy, as philosophy is for faith. Vd. Note 23 *supra*.

31. Vd. Carnap, *The Logical Syntax of Language*, New York, 1937; Reichenbach, *Experience and Prediction*, Chicago, 1938; Ayer, *Language, Truth and Logic*, London, 1936. For contemporary criticism of the doctrine of logical positivism, vd. Weinberg, *An Examination of Logical Positivism*, New York, 1937; Ewing, Meaninglessness, (Mind, XLVI, 183: pp. 347-364.)

32. Vd. *What Man Has Made of Man*, Lect. I; cf. Maritain, *Introduction to Philosophy*, Ch. VIII on "Philosophy and Common Sense", esp. pp. 136-137. By common sense, Maritain elsewhere points out, is meant "the intuition of first principles and the first certitudes which, like a dowry bestowed by nature, attend on the spontaneous exercise of reason. This common sense as natural *intellection* must be carefully distinguished from the common sense of primitive *imagery*, which conceives the earth as flat, the sun as revolving round the earth, height and depth as absolute properties of space, etc., and has no philosophical value whatsoever" (*St. Thomas Aquinas*, p. 165 fn.). Thus, for in-

stance, the intuitive inductions from the evidence of the senses that there is motion or change in the universe, that physical things come to be and pass away, that nothing can act upon another thing unless it is itself actual in some way, are items of common sense knowledge which every man possesses, though perhaps not in this verbalized form, purified of accidental imagery. Thus, for instance, the ordinary man may state the last of these inductions by saying that he knows that mere possibilities can't hurt him physically. Inductions of this sort, which the philosopher shares with the man of common sense and ordinary experience are the basic facts from which philosophical analysis proceeds. These are "first principles" in the sense of starting points of analysis, though not in that other sense of "first principles" which means the ultimate terms to which analysis reduces all explanations of the facts. Cf. Maritain, *Introduction to Philosophy,* pp. 118-119.

33. Vd. Rousselot, *op. cit.,* pp. 111-132. Cf. Maritain, *La Philosophie de la Nature,* Paris, 1935: pp. 132 ff.

34. No point needs to be reiterated more often than that there is nothing *a priori* about philosophical knowledge. The charge of *a priorism,* so frequently made today, applies justly to Descartes, but in no way to St. Thomas, as a philosopher. Every criticism which Locke directed against these crucial errors of Descartes, St. Thomas had formulated before him as outstanding canons of

philosophical method. This can be briefly indicated in two ways: first, that St. Thomas always proceeds from a knowledge of sensible accidents, what Locke later called simple ideas, to a knowledge of properties and intelligible natures, in the case of both physical and spiritual things. Thus, "substantial forms, which in themselves are unknown to us, are known by their accidents" (*Summa Theologica,* I,Q.77,A.1,ad.7). St. Thomas's position with respect to our knowledge of substances should be compared with the famous passage in Locke's *Essay,* Bk. II, Ch. 23. Vd. Rousselot, *op. cit.,* pp. 103-104. In the same way, our knowledge of the soul and its powers, of God and his attributes, is entirely *a posteriori,* from operations or from effects, which are immediate objects of sensitive apprehension. Second, St. Thomas everywhere distinguishes between knowing *that* and knowing *what;* and in many cases our *a posteriori* mode of knowledge carries us *demonstratively* no further than *that something is,* as the existence of matter or of God. *What it is* we can know only analogically, not demonstratively; but the analogical mode of knowing is also *a posteriori,* by remotion from sensible experience through negations and comparisons. Vd. *Summa Theologica,* I, QQ. 84-88. Cf. Maritain, *Introduction to Philosophy,* pp. 118 ff., 141 ff.

It is unfortunate that the good work of Locke in undoing the damage philosophy suffered at the hands of Descartes should have been, in turn, undone by Kant who, in order to avoid the consequences of Hume, set up another kind of *a priorism.* (Vd. Gilson, *Unity of Philosophical Experience,* pp. 165 ff.; 214 ff.; 223 ff.) The philosophy of St. Thomas is as much opposed to the *a priorism* of Kant as to that of Descartes, and essentially agrees with the empiricism of Locke, apart from some of its inadequacies through failure to distinguish intellect properly from senses. Vd. Note 61, *infra.*

35. In fact, there is no deception here, no need to speak "as if." The most general concepts of metaphysics are part of the natural equipment of human intelligence. By "principle" we mean either a concept or the propositions in which that concept is involved. The "first principles" of metaphysics are, then, its basic concepts, its ultimate propositions. These first principles are first both in the temporal order of analysis and in the logical order of resolution. Thus, most men thinking about the world of change employ such concepts as possibility and actuality, simple and composite, whole and part, substance and accident, one and many, perfect and imperfect, etc. They are using metaphysical concepts without knowing it. Let us appeal to these concepts as they occur in common discourse about changing things. After their presence is explicitly recognized, and they are seen to be indispensable to any intelligent account of phenomena, it is time enough to pass to definite formulations and explications of the concepts themselves. Thus, instead of bewildering our con-

temporaries by what seem to them airy references to Being and the First Principles of Metaphysics, we should be leading them gradually from the philosophy of nature, which employs metaphysical ideas, to metaphysics in which those principles are examined.

36. Not only is the philosophy of nature the proper place to begin with the gentiles, but it is also the locus of the most urgent need for constructive philosophizing today. "The task which lies before (us) is to disengage from the enormous contribution which the experimental sciences have accumulated in the past four centuries, a genuine philosophy of nature" (Maritain, *St. Thomas Aquinas,* p. 12). Cf. Gilson, *Le Réalisme Méthodique,* Paris, 1935: III, on La Spécificité de L'Ordre Philosophique.

37. Vd. Note 18 *supra.* It is similarly necessary to distinguish different sorts of adversaries in philosophy. "Metaphysics can dispute with one who denies its principles, if only the opponent will make some concession; but if he concede nothing, it can have no dispute with him, though it can answer his objections" (*Summa Theologica,* I,Q.1,A.8).

38. "We shall first of all endeavor to declare that truth which is the object of faith's confession and of reason's researches, by adducing arguments both demonstrative and probable, some of which we have gathered from the writings of the philosophers and of holy men, so as thereby to confirm

the truth and convince our opponents. After this, so as to proceed from the more to the less manifest, we shall with God's help proceed to declare that truth which surpasses reason, by refuting the arguments of our opponents, and by setting forth the truth of faith by means of probable arguments and authority" (*Summa Contra Gentiles,* I, 9).

39. If the question be asked, Which of these three problems is gravest? it can be answered by analogy with the way in which St. Thomas shows that, in one respect, the unbelief of heretics is more grievous than that of Jews and pagans because they believe more than these others; whereas, in another respect, the gravity of the unbelief of pagans is greater because more extensive. "Speaking absolutely," he concludes, "the unbelief of heretics is the worst" (*Summa Theologica,* II-II, Q.10, A.6). Cf. *ibid.,* Q.10, A.5. It would follow, therefore, from the point of view of theology, that it is more important to correct heresy than to convert infidels. But the difference between theology and philosophy requires an inversion here. The opposition to philosophy on the part of positivists and systematists is more grievous than errors within philosophy itself. Our order of problems is determined accordingly. Cf. Note 38 *supra.*

40. If the system is properly mathematical, the choice of postulates and definitions is dictated by the problems to be solved, the constructions to be made, the order to be introduced. But if it is a philosophical system, which is only cryptically a

system, the choice may pretend to have intellectual origins but it will more frequently confess its wilfulness. The notion that there are diverse systems of philosophy is, therefore, intimately related to the position that the plurality of philosophies reflects a diversity in temperaments expressing themselves in acts of the will to believe, tender-minded and tough-minded philosophies, radical and conservative philosophies, or, in the current idiom, democratic and fascistic philosophies. But no one has ever suggested that the different non-Euclidean geometries, for instance, could be so described. This is one way of indicating the error of the systematists in attempting to assimilate philosophy to mathematics in both subject-matter and method.

41. Vd. *Metaphysics,* I, 9, in which Aristotle criticizes the Pythagoreans and Platonists for assimilating philosophy to mathematics. "Mathematics," he says, "has come to be the whole of philosophy for modern thinkers, though they say it should be studied for the sake of other things" (at 992b).

42. The only two eminent philosophers who ever even tried to construct a quasi-mathematical system of philosophy were Descartes and Spinoza, Descartes imitating Euclid, and Spinoza imitating Descartes. Not only did they fail formally in the sense of misusing a form not applicable to their subject-matter, but their effort to achieve "rigorous mathematical deductions" in philosophy resulted in fallacious arguments and a rigor which tortured and killed whatever sound philosophical

sense they had. Vd. Gilson, *The Unity of Philosophical Experience,* Ch. V on Cartesian Mathematicism, esp. pp. 142-145. Also, A. E. Taylor, Some Inconsistencies in Spinozism, in Mind, XLVI, 182, 183.

St. Thomas has no more a *system* of philosophy than Shakespeare has a point of view or a message. In Shakespeare's poetry nature is imitated so well, so properly, that all the wide world is presented to us with artistic objectivity. So, too, in the philosophy of St. Thomas the world is laid before us; his thought about it is diaphanous, a perfect medium of vision. In both cases, the art conceals itself by performing its task so well. And in both cases, the art introduces order and proportion into a vast multiplicity of things. Let us not confuse the notion of "system" with the more general ideal of a good arrangement of parts. System in the mathematical sense is rigid, selective, exclusive: it has the kind of artificiality which is appropriate only to mathematical objects; but where mathematics deals with the ideal and the possible, philosophy deals with the real and the actual. The real can be ordered by art without distortion; it cannot be systematized.

"Matchless in its coherence, closely knit in all its parts as it is, Thomism is nevertheless not what we call a 'system'. When one says that it is distinguished from all other philosophical doctrines by its universalism, this must not be taken as a simple differentiation of extent, but rather as one of nature. The word 'system' evokes the idea of a mechanical connection or of a more or less spatial assemblage of component parts, and consequently a choice which, if not arbitrary, is at least personal, as it is in all artificial constructions. A system unfolds or progresses from piece to piece, starting from its initial elements. On the other hand, it is the essential demand of Thomism that all construction and mechanism should be rigorously subordinated to the immanent activity and vital movement of intellection: it is not a system, an *artefactum;* it is a spiritual organism. Its internal links are the vital connections by which each part lives by the life of the whole" (Maritain, *The Degrees of Knowledge,* New York, 1938: p. xiv).

43. *The Unity of Philosophical Experience,* p. 317. "For us, as for them," Gilson goes on to say, "the great thing is not to achieve a system of the world as if being could be deduced from thought, but to relate reality, as we know it, to the permanent principles in whose light all the changing problems of science, of ethics and of art have to be solved. A metaphysics of existence cannot be a system wherewith to get rid of philosophy, it is an always open inquiry . . . ." (Cf. W. Jaeger, *Aristotle,* New York, 1934: pp. 373-376).

And Maritain: "The truth is that Thomism is a universal work. One is not a thomist because one has chosen it in the emporium of systems as one among several others, as one may tentatively choose a pair of shoes at a bootmakers until one sees another brand more suited to one's feet. On those lines, it would be more stimulating to fabricate one's own system, made to one's own measure. One is a thomist because one has abandoned the attempt to find in a system fabricated by one individual, that individual who is called *Ego,* philosophic truth, and because one intends to seek for the truth,—albeit by oneself and by one's own reason,—learning from every form of human thought, so that nothing that is may be neglected." (*The Degrees of Knowledge*, p. xv).

44. *Ibid.,* p. 318. The very meaning of the word "perennial" makes the notion of a *finished* perennial philosophy self-contradictory.

45. It should be noted here that in the account of the intellectual virtues, there is no habit of concepts. The habit of understanding is the habit of propositions, self-evident because known immediately and naturally upon the possession of their terms. Just as the conclusion of reasoning explicates knowledge which is implicit in its premises, so the proposition *per se nota* explicates knowledge which is implicit in its concepts. To say that a self-evident proposition is a tautology is, therefore, to make two points: first, that it is genuine knowledge in so far as its component concepts are acts of understanding; second, that it is non-instructive only in the sense that it adds explication rather than novelty to what is contained in the concepts. The modern meaning of tautology neglects the first of these points and, therefore,

stresses only the non-instructive aspect of the judgment, the lack of novelty. Vd. Locke, *Essay Concerning Human Understanding,* IV, 7, 8. Add to this a touch of nominalism, and the judgment becomes verbal and arbitrary, the magician's trick of pulling the rabbit out of the hat. In the same way, the modern view of reasoning treats the conclusion as tautological because it is contained implicitly in the premises. The germ of truth in the modern view is that both judgment and ratiocination are due to the weakness of man's intellect; rationality is discursive and signifies intellectual defect. Both the judgment and the syllogism are substitutes which men must use for the wholeness of vision, the unity of intuition. That the first act of understanding, the having of concepts, is not for men a perfect act of knowledge indicates the low grade of our intelligence, and explains the tautological character of the judgments and reasonings which are needed to complete what men otherwise imperfectly apprehend. Vd. Rousselot, *The Intellectualism of St. Thomas,* Ch. II, IV. Cf. A. E. Taylor, *Philosophical Studies,* pp. 385 ff.; and F. H. Bradley, *The Principles of Logic,* II, pp. 622-641.

46. Like tautology, circularity in reasoning is a substitute for the immediate perfection of intuition. Circular reasoning approximates intellection; it is a way of gaining something like the center of an embracing vision. What we are unable to comprehend in a single act, we seek to apprehend

in a number of operations so ordered to one another that there is absolutely no beginning or end, but only relatively. As circular motion approximates rest better than the rectilinear, so circular reasoning is nearer to vision than linear inference. "Reason differs from intellect," St. Thomas tells us, "as does the multiple from unity; according to Boethius, its relation to intellect is that of the circumference of a circle to the centre, or of time to eternity. It is characteristic of reason that it traverses the ground around a number of objects in its effort to obtain a simple knowledge of them" (*In Librum Boetii de Trinitate,* Q.6, A.1). That St. Thomas's philosophy exemplifies this approximation to intellection, in its many circles of reasoning, shows him to be the *angelic* doctor, not the *subtle* doctor. Those who try to avoid such circularity in philosophy, from the mistaken notion that every circle is a vicious one, force their thought into the superficial channels of asymmetrical deduction, and cannot in the end escape subtleties which are truly vicious because deceptive. Vd. Sertillanges, *op. cit.,* p. 68, 81.

47. I would, in fact, maintain that the logic of philosophical knowledge has never been adequately formulated. The *Organon* of Aristotle presents the logic of philosophy in so far as it treats of predication in general, in terms of the predicaments and predicables. But the analysis of syllogisms,—of the moods and figures as determined by the accident of quantity,—deals with

modes of reasoning which seldom occur in the philosophy of nature and never in metaphysics; and the account of the structure of "science" in the *Posterior Analytics* almost suggests the mathematical notion of system and deductive development. Contrary to the view that Aristotle's logic reveals his biological interests, the *Posterior Analytics* shows the misleading influence of mathematics. Wherever mathematics is taken as the ideal of scientific exposition, the logic which results is too rational and not intellectual enough. It is only when reasoning is treated as a substitute for, and an approximation to, understanding, that the logic of philosophy is grasped. Plato made this clear in his distinction between the ascending dialectic of metaphysics and the descending dialectic of mathematics. And, curiously enough, it is in the *Topics* that Aristotle comes nearest to giving an account of the method of the philosopher, a method which Aristotle himself brilliantly exemplifies in his own philosophical works. The *Posterior Analytics* is a much better description of Euclid's *Elements* than of Aristotle's *Physics* or *Metaphysics*. Modern mathematical or symbolic logic is even more irrelevant to the structure of philosophical knowledge than the *Organon* of Aristotle.

48. In the first place, it is necessary to distinguish between philosophical and theological mysteries. The former are reached through reasoning, independent of Revelation. Vd. Garrigou-Lagrange,

God: His Existence and Nature, St. Louis, 1936: II, p. 197 ff. In the second place, we must recognize the good and bad meaning of the word "antinomy": antinomies which reason can and should avoid are contradictions which invalidate a philosophy, but antinomies which are inevitable, obscurities which the best reasoning leads to and cannot avoid, signify ultimate mysteries. Vd. *ibid.,* pp. 88 ff.; 197-202. It is only the rationalist, such as Spinoza and Hegel, who pretends there are no mysteries, not the intellectualist in the sense in which Rousselot describes St. Thomas. The best human knowledge, says Maritain, "does not destroy the *mystery* of things, that in them which is still unknown and unfathomed; but on the contrary recognizes and delimits it" (*Introduction to Philosophy,* p. 142) ; and elsewhere he writes: "There can in fact be no mystery where there is *nothing to know;* mystery exists where there is *more to be known* than is offered to our apprehension" (*Art and Scholasticism,* New York, 1930: pp. 28-29 fn.). Cf. Sertillanges, *op. cit.,* pp. 105-106, 113, 125; Gilson, *op. cit.,* pp. 108-109, 117.

In the third place, we must distinguish between two sorts of mysteries, those which are related to the infra-intelligible, such as matter and individuality and those which are related to the supra-intelligible, such as spirit and God. Vd. Garrigou-Lagrange, *Le Sens du Mystère et le Clair-Obscur Intellectuel,* Paris, 1934. In the fourth place, we must note the principle which separates the true antinomy from the apparent contradiction: in the case of the latter there is some falsity on both sides which can be eliminated in the resolution, but in the former there is, so far as human knowledge goes, truth on both sides. As the eminent mean position resolves a contradiction, so the recognition of mystery follows from what, for limited human understanding, are the apparently irreconcilable truths of the antinomy. VI. Note 57 *infra.*

Finally, in the light of these and many other considerations, we can understand why it is that philosophy, which begins with wonder, ends in awe. The love of wisdom is first aroused by the mystery of things, but reason can penetrate only so far, and the mystery and love of being terminate the quest. When man is so overwhelmed by mystery that he foregoes thought, a spurious mysticism results; when he is so determined to solve problems that he ignores mysteries, he undertakes to build a system from which he seeks to remove every contradiction. It is only when he distinguishes problems and mysteries, resolvable contradictions and genuine antinomies, that philosophy occurs. Cf. Dr. Gerald Phelan, *Jacques Maritain,* pp. 34-37.

49. At the joint meeting of the American Philosophical Association and the Catholic Philosophical Association, December, 1937, the point was made that the philosophy of St. Thomas was superior to that of Descartes, Spinoza, Hegel and other moderns because the latter ended in cul-de-sacs. The point was so poorly made that it could

be readily answered by the remark that so did the philosophy of St. Thomas run into a cul-de-sac. The discussion was fruitless because the distinction was not made between apparent contradictions, due to specious problems and the effort at system-building, and genuine antinomies, which indicate the area of mystery surrounding philosophy at its beginning and end.

Another error about antinomies, as I have pointed out, is the supposition that the reasoning which leads to an antinomy is thereby invalidated. This would require us to discard the faulty analysis and start from the beginning again. But the new analysis must come to the same end and be rejected. The life of thought would become a series of minor tragedies. (Professor Cohen speaks of Bradley's "high sensitiviness to the essential tragedy of human thought itself—its unavoidable task and its inescapable frustration." But he also says that "he was too robust a mind to suppose that the limitations of our intellect could enable us to dispense with it and run loose with vague words." In the New Republic, Sept. 30, 1925.) If, on the other hand, we realize that the antinomy does not make our reasoning infirm; if we hold to what we know as true, then the incomplete and fragmentary character of our truths, marked by the residual mysteries, ceases to be tragic and shows us our place in the divine comedy. We do not go back on our reasoning; rather it is thus that reason leads us to faith and the hope for vision.

50. The central effort of Gilson's William James Lectures was to expose the kind of *isms* which result from the substitution of other subject-matters and methods for those of philosophy. "It is a flat truism that all attempts to deal with philosophical problems from the point of view, or with the method, of any other discipline will inevitably result in the destruction of philosophy itself. Yet such abstract statements usually fail to convince those who hear them, and sometimes even those by whom they are made. One of the greatest uses of the history of philosophy is precisely that it brings us their experimental demonstration" (*Op. cit.,* p. 120). The historical evidence which Gilson assembles bears witness to the frustrations of grammaticism, logicism, theologism, psychologism, positivism or scientism. To this list might be added naturalism, or the exclusive predominance of physical questions in philosophy, and transcendentalism, or the exclusive predominance of the metaphysical. Furthermore, as I have tried to show in *What Man Has Made of Man,* these *isms* tend to become associated, as, for instance, positivism, psychologism and naturalism; or logicism, theologism and transcendentalism. And psychologism is often the route by which theologism leads to positivism. Cf. Gilson, *op. cit.,* pp. 68 ff.

51. Vd. Rousselot, *op. cit.,* Ch. III and V.

52. It is precisely because of his Christian faith and his subjection to sacred theology as *scientia rectrix* that St. Thomas is a better metaphysician than

Plato and Aristotle. "The natural weakness of man is incapable of attaining to the possession of the great truths of the natural order as a whole and without admixture of error, although each, considered separately, is within its range. We then realize that over and above the essential function of negative norm or external check before referred to, faith has also a positive office to fulfill in regard to philosophical reason, that is to indicate the goal and direct the mind, *veluti stella rectrix,* like a guiding star" (Maritain, *St. Thomas Aquinas,* p. 131). The negative function mentioned is regulative. Vd. *op. cit.,* pp. 129-130. Being merely philosophers, and not theologians in the sense in which St. Thomas could be one, Plato and Aristotle exemplify for us how even the greatest minds can transgress the limits of philosophy when reason is not rectified by faith; or, not transgressing, fall short of its fullest possible accomplishment. That Kant appears to be more critical than Plato and Aristotle is not a mark of greater genius in him but a tribute to the influence of Christian theology which reached him in however attenuated a form. To say, therefore, that St. Thomas is primarily a theologian implies not a dogmatic solution of philosophical problems but rather a surer and more guarded consideration of essentially philosophic themes. Vd. Sertillanges, *op. cit.,* p. 48, 83.

53. Gnosticism, in extreme forms, is a peculiar failing of modern philosophers because they are

Christians or have inherited the truths of the Christian tradition, without properly ordering reason and faith, philosophy and theology. It is different from mediaeval theologism in that the latter is due to theology swallowing up philosophy entirely. Modern gnosticism results from the efforts of thinkers to answer purely theological questions by merely natural means. The theodicy of Spinoza, the knowledge of the Absolute in Hegel, the discussion of the order of the universe in time and space by Whitehead, are examples of philosophy exceeding its domain. Though lacking faith, these philosophers do not seem able to regain the position of natural reason in Greek antiquity. Christianity has somehow been too much for them. When we learn that "Hegel's formative influences were theology and the classics," we can see the root of all his confusions. In a paradoxical sense, then, all modern philosophers are Christian, even when they are skeptical, as Hume, or agnostic, as Kant. Christianity has made problems for them which they cannot solve without faith, but which they will not refrain from discussing in rational terms.

54. The repetition of both errors and truths gives the history of philosophy its perplexing aspect to those who compare it with the history of science, in which error is corrected by truth and does not recur. Vd. the expansion of this point in *What Man Has Made of Man,* pp. 235-244.

55. These *isms* are of a different sort from those enumerated in Note 48 *supra.* There the source of error was the substitution of some other subject-matter or method for philosophy. Here the difficulty arises from the exclusive development of some partial truth as if it were the whole. The combinations and permutations of these two kinds of *isms* account for the *apparent* novelty of some of the errors which have occurred in modern thought. The possibilities are far from being yet exhausted.

As Gilson's Harvard lectures were an attempt to define the sphere of philosophy by a negation of *isms* of the first sort, so Maritain's *Introduction to Philosophy* strove to formulate the mean position between partially true extremes of philosophic doctrine. He showed how "on every one of the great problems of philosophy the doctrine of Aristotle and St. Thomas, when compared with the doctrines of other philosophers, appears as an eminence between two contrary errors. . . . The truth, indeed, is not to be found in a philosophy which keeps the mean between contrary errors by its mediocrity and by falling below then, being built up by borrowing from both, balancing one against another and mingling them by arbitrary choices made without the light of a guiding principle (*eclecticism*) ; it must be sought in a philosophy which keeps the mean between contrary errors by its superiority, dominating both, so that they appear as fragments fallen and severed from its unity. For it is clear that, if this philosophy be true, it must reveal in full what error sees only in part and distorted by a bias, and thus must judge and secure, by its own principles and in the light of its own truth, whatever truth error contains though it cannot distinguish" (*Op. cit.,* p. 270). The mean is eminent only when it is extreme. "Virtue, if regarded in its essence, is a mean state, but if regarded from the point of view of the highest good, or of excellence, it is an extreme" (*Nichomacheam Ethics,* II,6). Cf. Note 57 *infra.*

But Maritain's excellent summary is hardly an introduction to philosophy for those who are still gentiles in the sense of being outside the sphere of philosophy itself. Nor can it be for heretics. A text-book, however fine, is certainly not proportionate to the task of arguing with heretics. Even the students who are instructed by it will not be prepared sufficiently for that task. Vd. Maritain's discussion of the two ways of studying the philosophy of St. Thomas, in *St. Thomas Aquinas,* pp. 120 ff.

56. "Now truth apprehended by our intellect, if we consider it absolutely, is measured by things; since things are the measure of our intellect, as stated in *Meta.* X,5; because there is truth in what we think or say, according as the thing is so or not. Accordingly the good of speculative intellectual virtue consists in a certain mean, by way of conformity with things themselves, in so far as the intellect expresses them as being what they are or

as not being what they are not: and it is in this that the nature of truth consists. There will be excess if something false is affirmed, as though something were, which in reality is not; and there will be deficiency if something is falsely denied, and declared to be not, whereas in reality it is" (*Summa Theologica,* I-II,Q.64,A.3). What is to be emphasized here is that a person does not have intellectual virtue through any sort of "good operation," but only that sort which means possession of the truth. It can further be seen how dogmatism or gnosticism names the vice of excess, in affirming that that which is not, is; and how skepticism or agnosticism names the vice of defect, in denying that that which is, is. This is a generalization of their usual meaning which applies to undue extensions or contractions of the realm of knowledge itself.

57. "As Pascal saw so clearly, it is the mediocrity of our intellectual capacity in the first place which makes us fall into error, because we are incapable of comprehending simultaneously apparently opposite truths which are in reality complementary" (Maritain, *St. Thomas Aquinas,* p. 98). "In agreement with the rule of Pascal," says Sertillanges, St. Thomas "never discussed a truth without taking into consideration the opposite truth. . . . His mind, like that of his master Aristotle, oscillated between the *pros* and *cons* of a question, and finally dominated them all. Ideas that seemed to conflict when in shadow, he showed to agree

when brought into the full light of day" (*Op. cit.*, p. 68). Cf. *ibid.*, p. 62 ff; 68 ff.

It is the incorrigible mediocrity of the *specific* human intellect which makes antinomies inevitable in the best philosophy, just as in poorer thought it is the regrettable and remediable mediocrity of the the *individual* mind which is the source of error, i.e., avoidable contradictions. Vd. Note 48 *supra.*

58. *Commentary on the Summa Theologica,* at II-II,148, 4, *in finem.*

59. As A. E. Taylor points out, the philosophy of St. Thomas surpasses the wisdom of Plato and Aristotle because it supplements the inadequacy of each, resulting from the omission of the insight of the other. (Vd. Note 5 *supra.*) Leaning on Jaeger's scholarship, he distinguishes several strains in Aristotle: the more Platonic strain of the earlier texts, and the more scientific or naturalistic tendency of later ones. "Now there cannot be the slightest doubt that it is Aristotle in what seems to be earlier vein, the Platonic Aristotle, who means so much to Thomas" (*Op. cit.,* p. 249). In fact, the effort which Aristotle himself made to hold to the truths he learned from Plato, while at the same time correcting their excesses and supplementing their lack, is the effort which St. Thomas brought to fruition. "Here, as it seems to me, the so-called Aristotelianism of Thomas is much more thoroughly thought out and coherent than what I may call the Aristotelianism of Aristotle" (*Op. cit.,* p .246). On the other hand,

Taylor insists, against the usual notion that Thomas rejected Plato for Aristotle, that it is "at least an ambiguous statement to say that Thomas directly opposes Platonism in metaphysics at all. He certainly opposes particular doctrines of the *Platonici,* but it is another question whether he can be said to oppose the doctrines of Plato. (I am speaking, of course, of the Platonic metaphysics; I do not refer to psychology and the theory of knowledge, where we all know that Thomism is definitely Aristotelian)" (*Op. cit.,* p. 240). The point that Professor Taylor is making can be summarized in the statement that Platonism and Aristotelianism can be regarded as extremes, extremes of idealism and realism, of theologism and naturalism, which are properly mediated by St. Thomas by virtue of his being at once a better theologian than Plato and as much of a natural philosopher as Aristotle. Cf. Rousselot, *op. cit.,* p. 68; Sertillanges, *op. cit.,* pp. 47-48, 103, 122.

60. In this connection, one point must be made about the usual remark that St. Thomas is an Aristotelian. As Professor Taylor says, "in using such unqualified expressions there is the danger of creating a thoroughly false impression. There is one sense in which Thomas is no follower of Aristotle nor of any other man. He never accepts a doctrine because it has been taught by a man with a famous name and an established reputation; what he accepts he accepts because he believes it

to be true, or if not absolutely and certainly true, the nearest approximation that can be made to the exact truth. . . . You will remember how explicitly this point is made in the annihilating critique of the Averroist doctrine about the 'unity of the intellect.' We are told there, as plainly as we could be told, that our real concern is not what Aristotle taught but what is true. If the Averroists could succeed in showing that their own exegesis of Aristotle is correct, that would be so much the worse for Aristotle, but none the better for Averroes" (*Op. cit.,* pp. 243-244). Cf. Maritain, *St. Thomas Aquinas,* pp. 99, 109; also *What Man Has Made of Man,* Note 38a.

61. "St. Thomas, by probing deeply into the intimate nature of knowledge and the peculiar life of the mind, founds upon reason more securely than any other philosopher,—as against positivism but yet making the fullest allowance for experience and as against idealism but yet making the fullest allowance for the immanent and constructive activity of the spirit,—the objectivity of knowledge, the rights and value of the science of being" (Maritain, *St. Thomas Aquinas,* pp. 62-63). He most certainly anticipates Locke's "plain historical method"; he distinguishes, before Kant, between the regulative and constitutive use of "the ideals of pure reason." But his agreement with Locke on the primacy of sensation in human knowledge does not prevent him from seeing the contribution of the intellect; and his agreement

with Kant is not limited to the dialectical exploration of antinomies as marking the boundaries of reason, but goes further in its development of reason's analogical knowledge of the *what,* where by *a posteriori* procedure we can know demonstratively only the *that.*

62. Vd. *What Man Has Made of Man,* Notes 16, 16a, 20b, 21, 39c. Cf. A. E. Taylor, *op. cit.,* p. 253.

63. Vd. A. E. Taylor, *op. cit.,* pp. 253-54; and *What Man Has Made of Man,* Notes 20b, 25, 47. Cf. F. H. Bradley, *Appearance and Reality* and William James, *The Pluralistic Universe.* Rousselot's account of *The Intellectualism of St. Thomas* helps us to be sympathetic toward the absolute idealist's dissatisfaction with discursive reason, but though it is a poor substitute for the knowledge of vision, it is all we have and can have in this life. Though fragmentary and productive of ultimate antinomies, it is not, nevertheless, to be discarded as invalid or uninstructive, in favor of the idealist's paranoiac attempt to think himself into the sleep of experiencing the Absolute here and now.

64. "The daringly imaginative mind is apt to be deficient in sobriety of judgment, the emphatically sensible mind to be wanting in imaginative power. And, perhaps, when this is the case, since the object of philosophy is the attainment of truth, the thinker of really massive common sense, even

if his imagination is slower in its flights, really does more for philosophy than the dazzling but erratic and unsystematic speculator. The greatness of St. Thomas as a philosopher seems to me to lie in this, that his work combines high originality with an unsurpassed sobriety of judgment and sense for reality" (A. E. Taylor, *op. cit.,* p. 226). Cf. Sertillanges, *op. cit.,* pp. 4, 58, 84, 106. But in our account of his genius we must not forget the gifts which accompany faith. Vd. *Summa Theologica,* II-II, QQ. 8, 9. As Maritain says, "the secret both of his sanctity and his wisdom" is "the combination in him of the life of study and the life of prayer" (*St. Thomas Aquinas,* p. 114).

65. In Gilson's narration of the history of philosophy as a series of intellectual experiments, one point becomes intensely clear. The great philosophers are always better than their followers. In any period the formative thinkers are directly conversant with reality; in them philosophy begins with wonder about the mysteries of being or of knowledge. Their followers, however, are usually bookish men, finding problems in the texts of their master rather than deep in the nature of things. I do not mean that the formative mind need be unread, that originality can be bought only at the price of illiteracy; but rather that the great thinkers have made *some* tradition a part of themselves. Books are in the back of their minds as they face the facts of the world about them. The lesser disciples too often hold the book so

close before their eyes that they barely see the world around the edges. There are unfortunate consequences. A school of thought arises which lacks the vitality of its source; worse than that, the scholiasts attempt to smooth out the difficulties which the master left, the contradictions he failed to resolve, and in doing so fall to system-building with a vengeance. The master may have left inconsistencies in his work either because they were genuine antinomies or because in trying to be faithful to the realities he was looking at he was not willing to suppress truths which seemed to oppose each other. But unconcerned with those realities, and perplexed only by what they find in books, the followers lack the light to distinguish between ultimate mysteries and problems which can be solved. The work of Hobbes and Locke, of Kant and Hegel, is better for all the difficulties that are honestly and plainly there, than the work of their disciples trying to purify the texts. (Thus, it is better to impale Locke on the dilemma of ideas as knowledge of the real vs. ideas as objects of knowledge, than to do what Hume did, i.e., to take the second horn exclusively.) There is more truth in a large and rough attempt to think about the world than in the best system, shining with the polish of consistency.

Gilson summarizes all this in a single sentence: "There is more than one excuse for being a Descartes, but there is no excuse whatsoever for being a Cartesian" (*The Unity of Philosophical Experience,* p. 7). Must we not ask ourselves, therefore, whether we have any excuse for being Thomists? Must we not go further than Maritain, who says "there is a Thomist philosophy, there is no neo-Thomist philosophy" (*St. Thomas Aquinas,* p. 10), by adding there is not even a Thomist philosophy, but just philosophy? It seems to me that we must go to this extremity if there is any danger of our becoming bookish followers, neat and narrow-minded systematists. The danger is not fictitious, as much of the work done in the name of Thomism clearly shows. (Cf. Note 43 *supra.*)

There are three things which can help us to avoid the pitfalls which threaten any disciple. In the first place, if we understand why the philosophy of St. Thomas must not be regarded as a system, nor even as 'a philosophy,' but merely as an extraordinarily fine expression of philosophical thought, we should be able to do better than the followers of other masters who themselves thought they left great systems behind them. In the second place, if we can see why St. Thomas is not an Aristotelian, in the usual sense of that designation, we should be able to avoid being Thomists in the same way. (Vd. Note 60 *supra.*) And, finally, there is the difference between being the disciple of a tradition in which there is much truth rather than the inheritor of thought in which there is much error. As it was possible for St. Thomas to treat Aristotle as a good master without thereby becoming an Aristotelian, it is not similarly possible to treat Descartes without becoming a Cartesian, or Kant without becoming a

Kantian. "As though one could deal with error in the same way as with truth!" In short, if we succeed in being philosophers, acknowledging the leadership of St. Thomas and profiting by his help, the credit is largely due to the example he gives us to imitate and the truth he gives us to start with; but if we fail as followers and become Thomists instead of philosophers, the fault is ours. I owe to a friend the insight that it is not possible to be a good disciple of a false doctrine; but it must be added that it is not easy to be the good disciple of a true one.

66. For other statements of the programme of work to be done, vd. Sertillanges, *op. cit.,* pp. 139-150 and Maritain, *St. Thomas Aquinas,* pp. 124-125, 175. Vd. Note 16 *supra.*